Technology
and Literacy

Technology and Literacy
21st Century Library Programming for Children & Teens

**Jennifer Nelson
& Keith Braafladt**

AMERICAN LIBRARY ASSOCIATION
CHICAGO   2012

Jennifer Nelson is a passionate advocate for the role of public libraries as informal learning centers. She has over twenty-five years of experience working in libraries and has spent much of the last five years collaborating with the Science Museum of Minnesota developing sustainable practices for informal technology workshops for youth in public libraries. A frequent conference presenter on topics related to technology programming, youth, informal learning, and the future of public libraries, Jennifer holds a master's degree in political science and a master of library and information studies from the University of Wisconsin-Madison. She received her BA (magna cum laude) in political science from the State University of New York at Buffalo. She worked for over twenty years at the Minneapolis Public Library in a wide range of capacities and is currently senior grant writer at Project for Pride in Living, a Minneapolis-based nonprofit and library consultant.

Keith Braafladt is an experienced teacher and developer with a deep understanding of learners and the creation of learning environments in informal settings. Keith has a depth of experience with technology program implementation and spends considerable time developing effective curriculum for technology and media-infused classes and workshops. Keith's educational background is in fine art and museum practice. His work has focused on the intersection of art, technology, and science and how these integrate to support creative self-expression and social meaning making for adults and youth.

Printed in the United States of America

16 15 14 13 12   5 4 3 2 1

Extensive effort has gone into ensuring the reliability of the information in this book; however, the publisher makes no warranty, express or implied, with respect to the material contained herein.

ISBNs: 978-0-8389-1108-2 (paper); 978-0-8389-9418-4 (PDF). For more information on digital formats, visit the ALA Store at alastore.ala.org and select eEditions.

Library of Congress Cataloging-in-Publication Data
Nelson, Jennifer, 1961–
  Technology and literacy : 21st century library programming for children and teens / by Jennifer Nelson and Keith Braafladt.
    p. cm.
  Includes bibliographical references and index.
  ISBN 978-0-8389-1108-2 (alk. paper)
  1. Children's libraries—Activity programs. 2. Young adults' libraries—Activity programs. 3. Computer literacy—Study and teaching. 4. Technological literacy—Study and teaching. 5. Scratch (Computer program language) I. Braafladt, Keith. II. Title.
  Z718.3.N45 2012
  027.62′5—dc23
                                                                                    2011035104

Cover design by Kirstin Krutsch. Cover illustration © teacept/Shutterstock, Inc.
Text design in Fanwood and Melbourne by Casey Bayer.

♾ This paper meets the requirements of ANSI/NISO Z39.48–1992 (Permanence of Paper).

Contents

Acknowledgments

We would like to acknowledge the support provided by the Science Museum of Minnesota, the Hennepin County Library, and the Best Buy Children's Foundation that allowed us to develop this body of work. We would also like to thank our colleagues from across the country who were part of the Media MashUp project: Alicia Anderson, Rachael Bohn, Kelly Czarnecki, Jason Hyatt, John Lloyd, Zach Lutz, Cynthia Matthias, Brian Myers, Mahina Oshie, Hillary Pesson, Janet Piehl, Teresa Ramos, Aurora Sanchez, and Mary Seratt. Our work was supported in part by Media MashUp, a Nation of Leaders Demonstration Grant (NLG 07–08–0113) from the Institute of Museum and Library Services. Any views, findings, conclusions, or recommendations in this book do not necessarily reflect those of the Institute of Museum and Library Services.

Introduction

The inspiration for this work is best illustrated by retelling a story. In the fall of 2009 Jennifer had just purchased a snazzy new MacBook Pro. As she sat at home with her then twelve-year-old son, Henry, they embarked on a conversation that went something like this:

Henry: "Gee, mom, I bet they didn't have computers like these when you were a kid."

Jennifer: "Well, Hen, we didn't. I didn't use my first computer until I was in college. And when I started working at the library, the computer took up a room the size of our living room. And it couldn't do what our new one does."

Hen: "I bet when I get to be as old as you, they won't even have computers like our new one. I wonder what they'll be able to do. But I'm not worried about it because I'll figure it out."

In that sentence, Henry, in his twelve-year-year old wisdom, summed up the nature of technology adoption for the millennial generation: I'll figure it out.

He doesn't plan to need special training, and he's not worried about out how he'll adapt. He just knows he will. Now Henry is at a distinct advantage—his mom is a librarian, and his dad is a professor; he doesn't have to worry about where his next meal is coming from. We foster opportunities for him to experience new things and are fortunate that we can afford to do so. But not all kids have this luxury.

In 21st century America, kids still have variable access both to technology learning opportunities and to caring adults. The availability of these two resources can help ensure that all kids believe that they will be able to figure it out. And that's where public libraries can continue to make a difference in the lives of 21st century kids: by providing access and exposure to technology by library staff who are versed in the needs of 21st century learners.

In the following chapters we'll describe an approach to technology training for youth that is grounded in our belief that public libraries, today more than ever, have an important role to play in ensuring that kids of all stripes and in all locations are supported in developing key literacy skills that they will need to succeed in their lives.

This book is based on what Keith and Jennifer learned through a series of projects that took place between 2006 and 2010 which were supported generously by the Best Buy Children's Foundation, the Minneapolis Public Library, the Hennepin County Library, the Science Museum of Minnesota and its Learning Technologies Center, and the Institute of Museum and Library Services, through Media MashUp, a Nation of Leaders demonstration grant (NLG 07–08–0113).

Media MashUp was a project designed to test the adoption of rich media technology programs in a set of diverse public libraries. The project looked at several facets of program adoption: technology infrastructure, staffing, and the impact on youth. By most measures, the project was a success. Through the diligent work of staff at Hennepin County Library, Charlotte Mecklenburg Library, Free Library of Philadelphia, Seattle Public Library, Memphis Public Library, and the Wilmette (IL) Public Library, the project learned many lessons about how to navigate the sometimes rough waters of new program adoption. The technology workshops the project supported were largely based on a wonderful piece of software called Scratch (http://scratch.mit.edu), which is being developed by the Lifelong Kindergarten Group at Massachusetts Institute of Technology's Media Lab. Scratch is a wonderful tool for kids to create animation and media projects using a very simple and elegant programming language.

In this book we'll explain why we believe it is important for libraries to offer rich media technology-based programs for youth and how you can do it in your library. We'll share stories of our work and successful strategies we've developed. We know that the paths we've found aren't the only ones that will lead to success, but we hope that our stories will spark your interest in developing innovative and impactful programs for youth where you work. Chapters will provide a rationale and context for the shift toward technology-based youth programs as well as step-by-step instructions for developing Scratch-based workshops and classes.

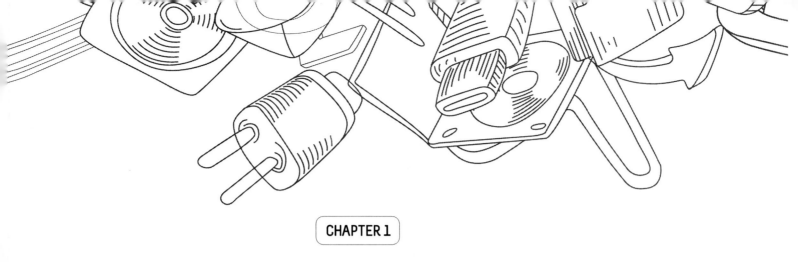

CHAPTER 1

Literacy, Public Libraries, and Education

To truly understand the important role that technology programming for youth can play in building stronger societies it's important to look at how young people learn today. Youth are entering a world that is vastly different from the one their parents were raised in, and the skills it takes to be successful have changed radically as well. The basis of our economy has shifted away from agriculture and factory work, and there are new understandings of what literacy skills are needed to be successful in work as well as to be civically engaged.

Over the last forty years or so, the American economy changed from a manufacturing and production-based economy to a knowledge-based economy.[1] With this wholesale shift in the structure of the economy has come a similar shift in the jobs created by the companies that drive it. Some economists have gone a step further and begun to identify a burgeoning conceptual economy.[2] The conceptual economy as described by Daniel Pink has six high-touch senses—design, story, empathy, symphony, play, and meaning—that are critical to success in the new world.[3] These new senses aren't in opposition to currently required skills and attributes. Instead, they are an enhancement of fundamental attributes we already possess. Other economists discuss the importance of creativity for continued economic vitality.[4]

As the nature of the economy has changed, so have the ways Americans experience their lives, their careers, and their work. This is a twofold change. First, the greatest number of jobs available is no longer in manufacturing, which required only on-the-job training to earn high wages. Most jobs are now created in the information/knowledge sector and require more sophisticated skill sets and more up-front education. Additionally, there is a growing stratification among workers, with jobs requiring either an advanced degree (medicine, law, engineering) or little to no extra training (entry-level health care or customer service).

The second change is in the number of jobs that individuals will hold in a career. Recent research from the U.S. Bureau of Labor Statistics shows that the average worker experiences ten job changes in a lifetime, far more than earlier generations. Derived from a longitudinal survey of late-stage baby boomers prior to the latest economic crisis, this observation is a likely indicator of future employment trends. This is particularly true given the increased number of business closings and consolidations. In the midst of this changing economic structure, the educational system has to produce kids who are flexible, adaptable, and, as Henry told Jennifer, able to "figure it out."

While the structure of the U.S. economy has undergone this dramatic shift, there has been a comparable social movement in understanding what literacy means in a computer- and Internet-driven world. Several organizations have developed approaches, or frameworks, for understanding literacy in the 21st century. Although they differ in some respects, there are several commonalities. All these frameworks recognize that technology skills are critically important, but not the mastery of skills in specific software applications. Rather, they argue the importance of an approach to learning with technology that involves critical thinking, higher-order problem solving, flexibility, creativity, and other related concepts.[5] These needs aren't developed strictly from a philosophical bent. They are developed from an understanding of the changing nature of work and employment that has been driven by the shift to a global economy. Literacy is now understood to encompass the traditional three Rs (reading, writing, and arithmetic) as well as a host of skills and attributes unique to the world in the 21st century. There are fine strands of literacy—media, digital, information, for example—as well as more encompassing frameworks that attempt to bring together all of what is needed to thrive in a modern society. The Metiri Group identifies *digital age literacy, inventive thinking, effective communication,* and *high productivity* as the hallmarks of 21st century literacy.[6] The Partnership for 21st Century Skills (P21) is another national initiative that has drawn positive attention and support for its work in redefining literacy. P21 uses an expanded framework that acknowledges the continued important role of reading, writing, math, and science and adds components that address technology and media fluency, interpersonal skills, and higher-order thinking and problem solving. In addition, it explicitly recognizes the importance of global awareness.

CONSTRUCTIONIST APPROACH TO LEARNING

Corresponding to this expanded understanding of literacy and the changed economy is the recognition that there are multiple ways that children can learn and build knowledge. The foundation for a new kind of thinking about how children learn is described in the *constructionist* approach rooted in the work of Jean Piaget and Seymour Papert. Applications for this approach have blossomed through the work of the Media Lab at the Massachusetts Institute of Technology (MIT), in particular the Lifelong Kindergarten Group. Similarly, as a society we've developed a better understanding of how children learn and how to best teach them. Mitch Resnick, for example, provides a nice discussion of learning that notes the importance to youth of connecting their life experiences with their learning and the importance of design thinking.[7] Although there are numerous approaches to learning that inform our work, none is more evident than Papert's work, particularly his articulation of a constructionist approach to learning in informal settings.

The constructionist approach to learning addresses the developmental needs of youth by incorporating the idea that we experience the deepest learning when we actually make things (construct learning artifacts) in a social setting. Learning is a social activity, and meaning is constructed by building. There are two ways to think about construction—knowledge is constructed through trial and error and through constructing objects in the real world, not just in the abstract in a classroom. The "show what you know" idea—that deep learning also happens when you have to explain projects you've built and demonstrate what you've learned—and technology workshops in libraries become tremendous opportunities for growth and learning. As an additional bonus, there is the good that comes from learning to speak in public.

In the world of 21st century education and learning, using computers to create things is a prime example of constructionism at work. Scratch (the software that is the basis for our approach to technology programming) is built on these constructionist foundations; hence its focus on supporting the development of fluency with media tools and computer programming while also addressing the 21st century literacy skills. Wrapping technology programming in 21st century public libraries with informal learning and a constructionist perspective on how learning takes place advances the whole idea of what a library can be. This is even more true when viewed through the lens of the developmental assets the library is nurturing.[8]

With this rich understanding, we can now turn to the question of how public libraries can best create the environment for this new learning and literacy to happen.

LITERACY AND THE PUBLIC LIBRARY

Public libraries in the United States have always been institutions where learning takes place. From the earliest days of the public library movement in the early 20th century to the beginning of the 21st century, learning has been an important component of library service. Another primary ethos in the development of public libraries is that they are free and open to all. Our collections, whether print, audio, or digital, are built around the goal of providing free access to information regardless of format so that learning is available to all.

Public libraries develop and offer classes and workshops to respond to a range of community needs. Early in the 20th century these programs ranged from providing English language learning for new immigrants to acting as a people's university where the unschooled had open access to literature on all subjects. Continuing in the 21st century, public libraries retain this practice of equitable service to all; with fewer membership requirements than any other educational organization, we truly serve all people in all of our communities. Over time, the types of programs and activities offered by public libraries have shifted as the needs of our communities have changed. As our knowledge about how people learn has grown and changed, the opportunities we offer and how we offer them have changed as well.

In particular, there has been tremendous change over the last hundred years in the forms in which information is contained, the tools with which it is accessed, and the skills needed to put it to use. Throughout most of the 20th century, reading was the primary skill that patrons needed to take advantage of the rich opportunities for learning that libraries offered. Today, with the advent of computers as tools for accessing information and building knowledge, our patrons need to have a skill set that goes beyond reading and includes a host of skills related to technology, digital fluency, media literacy, and more. Computers, the Internet, and various software applications have come to dominate how libraries operate and influence the services we provide. But the basic premise of what a public library can do (offer unfettered access to information) and how it serves its community (by identifying and responding to its needs) has remained constant.

The more than 16,600 public libraries in the United States are the heart of learning and informal education in America.[9] They have become our communities' primary center for informal learning, the place for accessing the tools of modern society—whether those tools are books or computers. Libraries are ubiquitous—they exist in virtually every community in the United States, rural, urban, suburban, exurban—and are an important constant. Libraries have supportive infrastructures that provide access to technology as a fundamental service. The concept of lifelong learning is expressed in the mission statement, goals, and priorities of many public libraries. The concept addresses the key public library role in informal learning and access to information technology.

The extent to which public libraries provide this basic access to computers and the Internet for the communities they serve is unrivaled by other organizations. Although some areas of the United States are fortunate to have community technology centers, most are without, particularly rural areas. Over 98 percent of public libraries offer computer and Internet access; more important, *71 percent of library users report that the library is their primary place for accessing computers and the Internet* [italics added].[10] A vast majority of these libraries offer broadband and high-speed access to the Internet.[11] These are critical functions as access to the Internet becomes essential for civic participation in 21st century America.

At the same time, libraries continue to provide support for literacy in all its forms; computers and software, like books, are tools for teaching and learning literacy.[12] And, of course, libraries strive to remain barrier free with no direct cost for membership. Our patrons (and their parents, teachers, grandparents, friends, and neighbors) have already paid for access. Public libraries require only respectful use of our space and resources. We remain important organizations in our communities, and our services complement those of the civic, recreational, and educational organizations that share our cities and towns.

Recognizing the changes in libraries, the Institute of Museum and Library Services (IMLS) has supported a range of projects that explore what it means to be a library in these times of radical change. Their work, through the Museums, Libraries, and 21st Century Skills initiative (www.imls.gov/about/21stCSkills.shtm), helps to shape the ways in which libraries respond to the tremendous changes in our communities.

LIBRARIES AS LEARNING CENTERS

Public libraries are a perfect place, and this is the perfect time, to develop, test, and offer educational technology programs for youth that are grounded in key literacy skill building—programs that fit between home and school and home and work. For today's youth, libraries provide many programs—homework support, book clubs, anime or manga clubs, and console gaming, to name a few—all of which fill those critical out-of-school-time hours. Just as technology is fast becoming the primary tool to support learning both inside and outside of school, libraries have an increasingly important role to play in providing access to these tools to youth who lack home resources. Public libraries have important choices to make in how we develop services and programs for youth. In addition to providing programs and learning opportunities at no cost, public libraries are free from externally imposed mandates related to what services are offered and how they are evaluated.[13]

The success of public schools is measured by the percentage of students passing required standardized tests, but there is no similar measure for libraries. Indeed public schools are in a quandary as their very funding is threatened by failure of students to perform at certain levels. Public libraries, on the other hand, have no such threats. This creates an immense opportunity for libraries to create a niche that responds to the needs of our young customers and to apply a range of approaches to serve those needs. And while it is tempting to develop and build solely on the basis of what kids are interested in, we have a professional obligation to provide opportunities that build skills and provide opportunities for youth to grow and stretch as learners and leaders.

In this book we advocate for the development of technology-infused programs to support informal learning in public libraries. While we are concerned with just one aspect of informal learning, out-of-school-time programs for youth, we believe this approach is relevant for how we serve all audiences for the 21st century.

Libraries are key community agencies, akin to science centers, history and children's museums and other organizations (Boys and Girls Clubs, YMCAs, for example) that provide out-of-school-time activities for youth. All of these organizations use an informal approach to learning. Note that we use the term *informal learning* rather than the more commonly used *lifelong learning*. This may seem a subtle distinction, but although lifelong learning is important and denotes the role public libraries play for patrons of all ages, the term is so all-encompassing that it loses much of its meaning. It can mean just about anything to anyone and doesn't denote a particular approach, be it formal, informal, or experiential.

What we call things, how we label them, is important. The act of naming is powerful; a name sets up expectations and sends a message. Many libraries proclaim the concept of lifelong learning and education in their mission statements. But do we really know what it means? Using these terms also positions libraries in alignment with schools—institutions of formal learning. For example, the International Federation of Library Associations (IFLA) defines lifelong learning as "all purposeful learning activity undertaken on an ongoing basis with the aim of improving knowledge, skills and competence."[14]

Public libraries in the United States are unlikely to adopt a formal approach to learning—doing so would move us far beyond the current models of staffing and could create an entirely different focus for service. So naming, developing, and calling out an informal approach, we believe, sets libraries up for the greatest success, particularly in working with youth in out-of-school time.

Shifting the library's role to that of supporting informal learning allows us to establish standards more closely aligned with those of organizations such as museums, camps, and YM/WCAs. When we make this shift, we can create a tremendous opportunity to meet youth where they really are—intellectually, developmentally, and cognitively. The standards by which we develop our programs and measure our success are then relevant to the outcomes we hope to achieve. We are positioned to support a community of youth who are deeply engaged in learning with workshops and classes that expose them to a much wider range of important literacy skills.

Taking this approach also allows us to make the best use of staff and a range of techniques for teaching and learning. Most informal learning organizations employ a wide variety of strategies for engaging youth that are as much about social skill development as specific content. So although learning the techniques to be a teacher in a formal classroom setting is probably beyond the interest and capacity of libraries, adopting the practices of informal educators is not.

INFORMAL LEARNING

Throughout this book, we use the phrase *informal learning* to reflect a core set of beliefs about how to best teach in informal educational settings. A key difference between formal and informal settings is the outcomes that are expected for program participants. In a formal educational setting, the expectation is that learners will complete fixed objectives that can be measured and tested. Further, a specific thing will be learned, and that knowledge will continue to increase.

Formal education is most often classroom-based and takes place within an institution whose primary focus is structured education.[15] Teachers in formal settings are credentialed and trained to develop curriculum with learning outcomes that are aligned with specific educational standards, whether they be content-based or focused on helping kids to pass required tests. The dictates of formal education inherently limit not only what can be taught, but also how teaching is structured, because at the end of the classroom day success is measured by the learners' ability to demonstrate specific content knowledge or by formal examination.

In informal settings, the limitations are not better or worse, but simply different. Although educators are freed from the requirement to teach to curriculum or testing standards, it is absolutely necessary to have clear and defined learning outcomes in an informal educational setting. Outcomes must be meaningful for learners and must be carefully documented to provide feedback for both learners and educators. Public libraries can take a broader approach that takes into account both what we teach and how we teach. We can focus on providing a setting that builds developmental assets and 21st century skills. Because librarians don't need to be licensed and trained as teachers, we are free to use teaching methods that encourage collaboration among participants. We can help youth develop their leadership skills while they deepen their content knowledge.

As libraries begin to engage with the informal learning community, we can develop better tools and skills for monitoring and measuring our success. We can be strategic and gather meaningful data that can help us to market ourselves to our funding agencies.

As long as we continue to align ourselves only with schools and the formal educational setting, and as long as we try to build programs to support the formal requirements for schools, we tie our fates to the vagaries of state and federal mandates for educational success. Moreover, we lose the essence of what libraries can do: step into the third space between home and school, home and work, to provide creative and meaningful opportunities for learning that use a range of techniques and tools to meet the needs of the learner, not the curriculum or the mandates.

PROGRAMMING OPPORTUNITIES FOR INFORMAL LEARNING

Traditional library preschool storytimes are a perfect example of how to approach informal learning in public libraries.[16] Story times are presented as opportunities for children to gain exposure to key literacy skills—letter knowledge, narrative skills, print awareness—in myriad ways.[17] Some include music and dance or finger plays, or food, but all are grounded in key literacy practices and are designed to generate an interest in books, libraries, and reading. Story-time programs may be formulaic, but there is nothing inherently formal about them. Even though most are thematic, they are not designed to teach kids how to read or to teach them lessons related to the content. Holidays such as Thanksgiving and topics such as trucks or elephants may guide an actual story-time development; there are legions of guides to developing story times that ensure success by connecting to the needs of our patrons.

Story times were never about teaching kids to read; rather, they were developed to expose them to literacy practices in a safe setting and with a wider array of tools than most family could provide. Books weren't ubiquitous in homes in those days, just as computers aren't now. Public libraries didn't always offer story times for young children. In the 1940s and 1950s libraries responded to a growing body of educational research that identified a need for children entering school to be ready to read. The goals for the story times were much the same as they are today and include a desire to promote social skills in young children, again as a prelude to entering the system of formal education.

> In the 1940s and early 50s, librarians began to understand their value as a resource for children learning to read. Public libraries offered an early version of storytimes in the early 1940s as a response to the emerging theory of "reading readiness." Reading readiness was the theory that children needed to be mentally prepared for reading by being exposed to literature before being given physical books to read. . . . This wide-scale effort, which resulted in literacy-focused story hours for preschool-aged children nationwide, was the library's first step toward becoming a major player in early and emergent literacy.[18]

Today's story-time practitioners are largely children's librarians in public libraries. They are not reading teachers, nor are they required to take classes in reading beyond a children's literature course in library school. They aren't required to take additional training, yet providing story times has become almost a requirement for public libraries of any size. This is true despite the fact that an increasing number of organizations in a community—both large and independent bookstores, for example—now offer them as well. Libraries no longer own the market for story times, yet we have set the standard for a quality early literacy program. We've proven it works and now others in the community have adopted our practice.

Technology-infused programs for older youth, then, are simply story times for the 21st century—exposing kids to key literacy skills at a critical time in their lives.

As with story times, providing activities for school-age patrons is common in public libraries. The range of activities offered runs from in-person and online homework tutoring to console-based gaming programs, from teen advisory groups to book, anime, or game design clubs. Children and teen librarians are sensitive to the needs and interests of youth in designing programs. Many encourage youth to take an active role in designing programs, purchasing materials, and more. What is often lacking, however, are programs that are designed with clearly articulated goals and outcomes that are rooted in 21st century literacy skills such as collaboration, higher-order thinking, and problem solving.

Many out-of-school-time programs for youth are thoughtfully designed and developed, yet those in the library profession have had little exposure to creative and innovative program development within the context of formal, outcome-based planning. While the traditional ad hoc approach has served us well in the past, it will not serve us well in times of economic downturn nor allow us to develop responsively for our patrons in the future. With increasing threats to our economic viability, public libraries are called upon to demonstrate our value and our outcomes in ways that are unfamiliar and perhaps even uncomfortable. But without documentation of why we do what we do and what impact our efforts have had, individual libraries will be hard pressed to provide the data needed to justify their existence.

Kids already have opportunities to access and use technology in other areas of their lives, so why is it so important for libraries to offer youth-oriented programs and activities that incorporate information technology experiences and access? What does the public library offer that other organizations don't? Why is public library staff perfectly placed to make these connections for youth? What do the youth gain? What do the libraries gain? We will address these quesions in the following chapters.

TECHNOLOGY AND INFORMAL LEARNING

Our framework for youth technology workshops with an informal learning approach has two objectives. The first is providing intentional opportunities for youth to develop 21st century skills. The second is using the core principles of positive youth development, through the lens of Search Institute's Developmental Assets (www.search-institute.org/developmental-assets-are-free), as a way to respond to the developmental needs of youth.

Public libraries currently are in prime position to provide the external assets to help youth develop the internal assets so critical for lifelong success. Those external assets include defining the roles for staff as they empower youth, help them use their time constructively, and set (and enforce) appropriate boundaries.[19] Technology-based programs, with high appeal to youth, can help public libraries build developmental assets in youth in our communities. By doing so, we establish libraries as key partners with schools and families in building strong and safe communities. Library staff leading technology programs can be those additional supportive adults that youth need in their lives. Regular programming for youth, whether weekly or monthly, provides a structured opportunity for exploration as well as social and intellectual development.

As the role of public libraries shifts to support the changing information environment, fulfilling this need will only become more important. With concerted focus on this role, youth services librarians will begin to build deeper relationships with youth that can lead to positive outcomes not only for those served, but for the communities in which they live.

The kind of technology training that we advocate is not a Web 2.0 or even Web 3.0—a collection of online information application strategies or social media practices. Rather, it is a change in philosophy and training that is infused with a deep understanding of the changing nature of literacy and its importance for youth of today as they move into the workforce. Informal learning around technology is not synonymous with teaching Web 2.0 skills. Our focus is to create technology-based programs and environments for learning that foster developmental assets and champion creative thinking.[20] The informal learning approach transcends technology and is about creating intentional communities and opportunities around learning that lead to the development of 21st century skills. The goals of technology-based programming aren't much different from the goals of other library programming for youth. The skills that staff need to meet these goals—helping connect kids to one another in a caring and safe space with a healthy dose of literacy and learning—are much the same.

As our projects developed, we were delighted to see that the Scratch software (http://scratch.mit.edu) we had begun to incorporate in programs had been created with an eye toward these new realities. The Scratch team correlates several of the Partnership for 21st Century Skills to what Scratch teaches. The skills the team identify include communication and information/media literacy, problem identification, formulation and solution, creativity and intellectual curiosity, critical and systems thinking, interpersonal and collaborative skills, self-direction, accountability and adaptability, and, finally, social responsibility.[21] Our work in Media MashUp, gathered by observations of almost a hundred workshops, bears out much the same findings. Although not a scientifically valid sample size, the results are nevertheless notable. Based on these observations we learned that well over 60 percent of participating youth consistently demonstrated key 21st literacy skills: communication and collaborative skills (66 percent), creativity and innovation (71 percent), skills in information and communication technology (75 percent), productivity and accountability (73 percent).[22] Clearly, Scratch offers opportunities for youth to gain critical skills that will guide their future success in life.

NOTES

1. Lesley Southwick-Trask, "Building New Skills for the Knowledge Economy," *Business Communications Review* 26, no. 2 (February 1996): 28.

2. See, for example, *Wikipedia*, s.v."Conceptual Economy," http://en.wikipedia.org/wiki/Conceptual _economy.

3. Daniel Pink, *A Whole New Mind* (London: Riverhead Books, 2005).

4. New England Foundation for the Arts, " Strengthening the Creative Economy," www.nefa.org/what _we_do/strengthening_creative_economy; and Peter Coy, "The Creative Economy," *Businessweek Online* (August 28, 2000), www.businessweek.com/2000/00_35/b3696002.htm.

5. Partnership for 21st Century Skills, www.p21.org.

6. The enGauge list can be found at www.metiri.com/features.html.

7. Mitchel Resnick, "Learning by Designing," http://info.scratch.mit.edu/sites/infoscratch.media.mit .edu/docs/learning-by-designing.pdf.

8. Search Institute, "Developmental Assets," www.search-institute.org/developmental-assets.

9. American Library Association, "Number of Libraries in the United States," Fact Sheet 1, www.ala .org/ala/professionalresources/libfactsheets/alalibraryfactsheet01.cfm.

10. John Carlo Bertot et al., "Libraries Connect Communities 3: Public Library Funding and Technology Access Study 2007–2009," www.ala.org/ala/research/initiatives/plftas/index.cfm.

11. OCLC, Inc., "How Libraries Stack Up: 2010," www.oclc.org/reports/stackup/.

12. Jo Ann Ellingson, "21st Century Literacy: Libraries Must Lead," *American Libraries* (December 1998): 52–53. More recently, Christine Mackenzie reviews emerging themes in library service, "Emerging Themes for Public Libraries Looking Forward," *APLIS* 29, no. 11 (December 2009): 184–189.

13. Britt Marie Haggstrom, ed., "The Role of Libraries in Lifelong Learning" (final report of the International Federation of Library Associations and Institutions, 2004), http://archive.ifla.org/VII/ s8/proj/Lifelong-LearningReport.pdf.

14. Ibid.

15. One description of formal versus informal education can be found here: Corporation for Public Broadcasting, http://enhancinged.wgbh.org/started/what/formal.html; Sherry Hsi's research on 21st century kids and learning brings home the reality of life for kids today in "Conceptualizing Learning from the Everyday Activities of Digital Kids," *International Journal of Science Education* 29, no. 12 (October 2007): 1509–1529.

16. Judy MacLean, "Library Preschool Storytimes: Developing Early Literacy Skills in Children," 2008, www.ed.psu.edu/goodlinginstitute/pdf/fam_lit_cert_stud_work/Judy%20MacLean%20Library%20 Preschool%20Storytimes.pdf.

17. Renea Arnold and Nell Colburn, "The (Really) Big Six: Early Literacy Skills," *School Library Journal,* (November 1, 2008), www.schoollibraryjournal.com/article/CA6610494.html.

18. Meagan Albright et al., "The Evolution of Early Literacy: A History of Best Practices," *Children and Libraries* (Spring 2009): 13–18.

19. Search Institute, "Developmental Assets List," www.search-institute.org/developmental-assets/lists.

20. Mitchel Resnick, "All I Really Need to Know (About Creative Thinking) I Learned (by Studying How Children Learn) in Kindergarten," in *Proceedings of the Creativity and Cognition Conference,* Washington, DC, June 2007.

21. Natalie Rusk et al., "21st Century Learning Skills," http://info.scratch.mit.edu/sites/infoscratch .media.mit.edu/docs/Scratch-21stCenturySkills.pdf.

22. Jennifer R. Nelson et al., Media MashUp, unpublished data.

CHAPTER 2

Building Capacity for Innovative Program Development

nnovative library programs can start in many places. Creative staff may come back from a conference with new ideas, outside partners may bring you ideas for collaborative projects, and, most important, library patrons may request specific activities or classes. Good ideas that appeal to youth and have the potential to be highly engaging often come from diverse sources.

All libraries need a process for the thoughtful consideration of new program and service ideas. For some, new ideas may imply that there is something wrong with the current way of doing things. For others, proposed innovations in programs or practice can be seen as a threat, one that may divert already-scarce funding, staff, or resources from existing (and prized) programs and services. But without the capacity to develop new programs and services, libraries run the risk of falling behind their patrons' (and the organization's) needs; misunderstanding the realities of changing economic, political, and information environments; and becoming obsolete.

Innovation doesn't have to be expensive. It often has as much to do with changing existing attitudes as it does with adopting new or different practices. Adopting an innovative approach to services and programs doesn't necessarily mean that existing ones will be displaced or discontinued. Innovative thinking can define new areas for growth and actually create new opportunities, but this needs to happen in a thoughtful and reflective way. In fact, the best approach to innovation in libraries is an incremental one. Introducing a new project doesn't have to shake our services to their core. It can be a way to carefully pilot new ideas that can help us to address the growing needs of patrons and create a deeper partnership with our communities.

GAINING ORGANIZATIONAL SUPPORT

An organizational attitude that encourages small-scale design and testing will lay the groundwork for larger scale change that is based on solid experience. The relatively narrow focus of Media MashUp was on finding new ways to help youth build key literacy skills. The workshop approach was tested, modified, and adopted by participants. It provided a limited scale to test the capacity of libraries to create and sustain such programs. We purposefully built in the capacity for our partners to develop workshops on the basis of their library's existing resources and traditions in the hopes that each could be successful. When resources are limited or shrinking but demand stays the same or increases, it is hard to imagine doing anything other than the status quo. Yet we found that where risk taking is supported and passionate involvement in new ideas exists, change happens.

Remember, it's best to start small. Many libraries have mechanisms to support small-scale ($500–$1000) pilot projects. Seed money may come from an innovation line in an operating budget or from contributions from foundations and Friends organizations, which can be used for special projects or at the discretion of the director or designee. The Wilmette Public Library, for example, has an annual innovation competition and invites staff to submit projects for consideration. Each year the library's administration selects one project to fund. By positioning such programs as pilot projects you reduce concerns about sustainability, eliminating a familiar barrier to innovation.

Pilot projects are, by their nature, experiments. Media MashUp was designed as a pilot project to implement technology programming for youth in public libraries. Media MashUp had several goals: to see if youth would attend technology-based workshops, to see what teaching approach was most effective, and to determine the capacity of libraries to develop and execute the workshops. At the outset, we wondered whether the project would be sustainable. We weren't sure if we wanted to continue beyond the pilot project—much less deal with the mechanisms that would allow that to happen—but we knew that the inability to address sustainability could sink the project before it had a chance to succeed. We also knew we needed to allow for possible failure. There might be many of those; even most well-developed projects can fail. There might be many reasons for failure; poor planning shouldn't be one of them

GAINING ADMINISTRATIVE SUPPORT

It's important to engage the right people to guide new ideas through an organization. While it's tempting to label key players by department, it's more important to focus instead on identifying their functions. You want to know who has the most influence and who controls the purse strings. The players in technology programming include library leadership as well as information technology and public service personnel. Who do you need to engage from your library to get a pilot project off the ground? Here are some areas to consider.

Who buys the computers for your library? This is typically someone in the IT department but may vary depending on governance. A county library system, for example, may have all IT purchases run through the county's IT department. You need the support of the internal (to the library) and external person who can authorize purchases and advocate for your project's needs. There may be standard models of computers, for example, that are the only ones available to you. You need to know this kind of information before you get too far along in the planning process.

Who decides what classes, workshops, and programs your library develops and offers? Is it a youth services coordinator? A programming librarian who has oversight over any and all activities, regardless of audience? Depending on the size of your library it may be one person or several or even a team. Is there a regional library system or collaborative that develops and implements programming for member libraries? Do branches in your system make local decisions about what happens or is there centralized coordination? Are there local sources of funding for your branch or are all funds channeled through headquarters?

Who decides what kind of training staff in specific buildings receive and how staff can spend their time? Is in-building programming done only by local staff or are there staff who work across the system and provide standardized programming throughout all buildings? If you're thinking about taking your programs out to schools or other organizations, who manages those relationships and who decides? If your location can't support your interest in offering programs, can you bring them to another library location? And finally, who makes software purchases and image management decisions? This may be one and the same person.

Most library budgets are constrained in what software can be purchased and in how it is licensed and made available. At the Hennepin County Library, for example, there is a public technology applications team that is led by information technology staff and includes professional librarians and support staff that make recommendations for software to be added to the library's image, whether free or paid. The staff members include youth and adult services as well as technology assistants. At the Free Library of Philadelphia the image team is directed by collection services because in that organization software on the computer image is considered part of the library's collection. The representation of the team is similar to Hennepin's; the key difference is in placement within the organization's hierarchy.

These questions aren't meant to intimidate, but rather to point out the many paths to success and to assist in locating people in your organization who can advocate to get staff what they need to create interesting, relevant, and innovative approaches to service.

A library's decision on where to position a team relates in part to how funding is allocated and in part to the service provided. Collections and IT, it should be noted, are often kissing cousins in libraries, sharing a closer relationship to one another than to building management or public service staff. The key, of course, is to know how to work within the structure of your organization, or to make recommendations for how the decision-making process can be adapted to allow for more innovative projects to develop. Direct software cost is only one factor. The cost for free software, if it has to be uploaded on each individual workstation, may quickly become prohibitive—hence our focus on laptops.

If you're in a position to influence your organization's decision making or organizational structure, organizational charts from other libraries are a great source for identifying different ways to get things done. A quick Internet search for public library organizational charts will give you a better understanding of different ways libraries are structured. This, in turn, may give you ideas about how your organization can enhance its ability to develop innovative projects by giving a road map of different decision-making processes.

GAINING STAFF SUPPORT

Can library staff advocate for trying out new ideas in programming? You bet. We have summarized here some strategies that seem to work. It's tempting to say what we discovered are best practices, but our long experience tells us that the phrase sets up unrealistic expectations about success.

1. *Know your organization.* Learn who the key decision makers are. The ones most concerned with your project may not be those at the very top. They may be staff who stay behind the scenes and quietly move mountains, or a team or committee that gets things done more formally. A few watercooler conversations with key individuals might work wonders. Find out how others brought forward new projects and follow their lead.

2. *Build relationships thoughtfully.* Think about what key players need and what they should know to support your efforts. Listen to their questions and respond to their concerns. If information technology staff is worried that updating or adding new software will be complicated, find out how staff at a similar organization responded to the same issue and share this with your staff. Build bridges within your organization and between your organization and others. Be alert to hierarchy when working across organizational silos.

3. *Prepare a program outline and time line.* Consider everything carefully, even the smallest of issues. The time you spend in planning really pays off in the end. The trick is not to let the planning process overtake the implementation.

4. Ask colleagues you respect to review your plan. They can help you identify pitfalls in your thinking and areas that might get you in trouble. Respond to their feedback. Their suggestions can help you articulate what you're trying to accomplish and build the support network you'll need to flesh out your program plan and move ahead on it.

For example, when the Hennepin County Library decided it was interested in experimenting with video reference, two staff members developed a clear and concise proposal that identified a process for testing the service at a few locations first, before establishing it in a soon-to-open building. Their document was well written and clearly articulated the point of the first part of the project (to establish test equipment fidelity and customer interest), yet it initially failed to gain support.

The writers called what they were doing a *pilot project.* In reality the proposal had two distinct steps: a pretest activity, followed by a pilot project. Knowledgeable colleagues reviewed the plan and helped the writers to revise their proposal to present a two-step process that would allow staff to determine first if the project seemed likely to work, then to proceed with an actual pilot project to see if video reference would benefit customers and workflow.

5. Talk about your project early and often. But keep the message simple. The only people who need to know the nitty-gritty are the staff who will be helping with implementation. Develop your key messages and share them consistently. You might get bored saying the same thing over and over, but repetition is a proven way to spread the word about your plans. Be ready to point to other libraries that have done similar projects. Get some research on your side.

6. Be prepared to compromise. Have some thoughtful, creative alternatives handy. Demonstrating willingness to be flexible can often get you further toward your goal. For example, you may want to run a technology workshop that requires three pieces of expensive software be installed on ten computers in your lab. If that's not possible, can you still run the class with the software on only five? Maybe you can go forward with only two pieces of software. These compromises will change how you run the workshop, but if your program is important, they are worth making. Just have a clear idea from the start what can be negotiated without sacrificing the goals of the project or diminishing the experience you hope to provide the kids who attend the program.

7. Know the details. Be ready to answer questions. If you don't know the answer, explain that you will find out. Be responsive and timely! If you respond quickly, you are demonstrating the importance of the project in a very tangible way. You are your own best ally, and your ability to address the issues that are raised in a timely manner will be critical to your success.

8. *Don't waste time.* Prepare realistic meeting agendas, stick to the topics, and stay on task. Learn some techniques for running effective meetings and always follow up with a thank-you. Identify your next steps. [1] Then follow through on actions.

9. *Be smart about deadlines.* Create short-term deadlines and long-term milestones. Then stick to them. Hold yourself and your project partners accountable. By making the deadlines and the milestones available in a shared document,[2] you set up a collaborative tone. Also be realistic. Assume things will take longer than you expected, and multiply your estimate by the number of people, departments, or organizations involved. If possible, make adjustments ahead of time; rework your work plan and schedule as needed and communicate the changes clearly to everyone involved.

10. *Demonstrate your idea to everyone and anyone.* Set up a half-hour to hour-long demonstration and question-and-answer session. Bring in computers and give everyone a chance for a hands-on experience. Make the demonstration lesson fun and engaging. If possible, bring in teens to help out. It's hard to resist the appeal of earnest teens. Make your short lesson available to coworkers in both print and digital formats. They will get a better idea of what you want to achieve, and they will appreciate your attention to detail and your willingness to share. This is not trivial. If you are establishing good working models for developing and running programs, staff will be able to see how your practices can improve their work.

11. *Use laptops if possible.* Even small, inexpensive models will do (Scratch, for example, was designed to work well with smaller netbooks). Laptops allow flexibility in room setups to ensure the best possible learning environment; any meeting room or space can be used. They allow image software to be stored on a DVD and updated or changed quickly. They pose a minimal security threat to the library's internal operations because they need not be connected to a library's network. They are easier to acquire as they can often be purchased with outside funding or accepted as donations.

Handheld devices, smartphones, and tablet computers offer even more opportunities for affordable technology based programming and might actually support our patrons more efficiently and equitably. Many of the issues we've highlighted will help in making decisions about the use of these newer tools as they become available.

OUTCOME-BASED PLANNING

Media MashUp was developed using a formal outcome-based planning process. While it is tempting to preach the importance of outcome-based program planning and development, we're aware that engaging in this kind of detailed work isn't the norm in public libraries. We do recommend using a tool such as Shaping Outcomes (www.shapingoutcomes.org/course/index.htm),which was initially developed by a collaborative team from Indiana and Purdue Universities with funding from the Institute of Museum and Library Services, or the Kellogg Foundation's Logic Model Development Guide (www.wkkf.org/knowledge-center/resources/2010/Logic-Model-Development-Guide.aspx) as part of the planning or implementation process of any library program.

It is challenging to track outcomes for library programs. There is a disparity in how the word *program* is used by public libraries as compared to how it is used by other organizations that serve youth and by researchers. In public libraries, the term program (small p) refers to one-time or periodic events or activities that are not designed to be repeated or to routinely draw the same audience. In other out-of-school-time organizations, the term program (big P) refers to an overarching approach to serving youth that may have several facets. An out-of-school-time big P program for youth may run five days a week for three hours daily with the expectation that kids are signed up in advance and will consistently return. The range of activities the program comprises might include homework help, physical activity, field trips, and other kinds of activities. Since outcomes (actual changes in attitudes or behavior) can be measured only over the long term and only in individual participants, library programs, as they currently happen, will not be successful in such measures.

However, the benefits of using outcome-based planning transcend the issue of measurement. We can still build quality programs that have a short-term and positive impact on youth. This approach allows the planners to deeply consider the purpose of the project, the available resources, and its desired outcomes. This, in turn, creates a common language that can be used to talk to administrators or funding agencies.

The planning process for Media MashUp led to several goals for the project, that are summarized here:

- Assess the capacity of each library to adopt a particular type of technology programming.
- Assess the learning outcomes related to 21st century skills that youth develop through participating in the workshops.
- Test two workshop models to see which was more successful with youth.
- Assess the capacity of staff to develop skills to lead workshops.

All of the libraries participating in the project were interested in the larger goals of the project, but different factors led to successful implementation of workshops at each location. Common among them was the presence of a larger organizational purpose that provides direction for innovative development, whether the driving force was technology, working with youth, or working with partner organizations.

Each model reflected the staffing, technology, and funding realities of the individual library. We found that money, in and of itself, didn't lead to success. Rather, success was achieved through thoughtful planning and a sound rationale that explained the importance of the project. These factors, in addition to a passionate staff, were the key ingredients. Additional funds helped, of course, but at the close of the project most of the libraries were planning to continue offering workshops even in the absence of grant funding.

CASE STUDIES

To successfully offer technology programs for youth at your library, you will need to be opportunistic—to take advantage of any and all help, both inside the library and out. Three of the participating Media MashUp libraries—the Free Library of Philadelphia, the Memphis Public Library, and the Seattle Public Library—were particularly skilled at this.

Memphis was able to leverage a partnership with the local Society for Information Management to obtain several recycled laptops. Library reference staff (with skills obtained outside the library) created their own workstations using open source software. It did not work perfectly, but it did allow the library to run the workshops in a financially stressed organization, and to do so in a sustainable way. Connecting the laptops to the wireless network, for example, was problematic; connections were poor and inconsistent in the primary program room. Staff sometimes had to switch gears in the midst of a workshop and use flash drives to capture projects on the fly to upload later.

Memphis also used funds from the Memphis Library Foundation to purchase additional technology tools (PICO boards, for example) for workshops that provided an extension to the basic workshops, which was a nice hands-on experience for youth. Memphis scheduled most of the formal workshops as part of its existing Tech Week Camp during the summer. This allowed them to reach a dedicated audience of thirty kids for thirty hours during one exhausting summer week. A small group of participants continued to attend informal workshops after the close of the camp. Their success in reaching kids through this project encouraged them to expand beyond the initial location to others in the system.

The Free Library of Philadelphia has a long-standing approach to programming that makes good use of its active foundation and its partnerships with local colleges. The Free Library employs dedicated program staff that regularly engage college students to work in local branches and to try out new programs. In addition to inexpensive laptops and other tools provided by the foundation, these college partnerships let the library offer more programs with enthusiastic and energetic interns. The interns were a wonderful source of creative energy. Providing college students as mentors for younger youth is especially appealing in areas where kids may need positive role models and clearly fits the desire to foster developmental asset building in youth.

The Seattle Public Library held some workshops in the library and collaborated with a local YMCA in an outreach capacity. Project staff leveraged an existing relationship with the program leaders and brought the workshops to the Y. Delivering programs outside of our buildings is an innovative way to deliver service that is just in time and has several pluses. There was a ready audience of kids who knew one another, making social interaction smooth. Staff from the Y made sure that the technology was ready to go and that the kid's behavior was well managed. This allowed library staff to concentrate on the fun part—teaching the kids to explore their creative ideas. It was a win-win situation for both organizations.

The best practice from these experiences is that it is critical to work across organizational silos and with cross-functional teams that can reach consensus about the direction for programs and projects. The ability to do this and move beyond personalities is enhanced with a strategic plan or set of overarching goals that can be the touchstone for any new projects. A sound strategic plan will allow innovation to flourish because it simply points the way to where we'd like to go and doesn't prescribe how we will get there.

Innovation approved, implementation begins.

NOTES

1. There are some great resources for running effective meetings, including "Running Effective Meetings," www.mindtools.com/CommSkll/RunningMeetings.htm.
2. Google Docs and Dropbox are two tools that internal and external partners can easily use to share documents of all kinds.

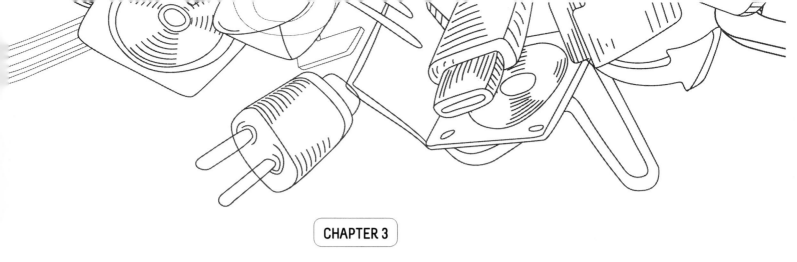

CHAPTER 3

Technology Programming Challenges and Opportunities

Bringing new and different programs to established organizations can be difficult. This is especially true for technology programs that by their nature cross all kinds of organizational boundaries and require coordinated efforts for success. The work we've done through Media MashUp has identified many challenges. Some are related to staffing (both time and skills), communication and marketing, and the cost of materials, while others are related to technology, network security, computer management, and availability of equipment and software.

There are also challenges related to changing the focus of library-based programs from books and reading to computers and technology-facilitated activities (such as interactive media, game development, or online content creation). This shift may not sit well with all staff, but as we've discussed, these new types of programs address key literacy skills for youth growing up in the 21st century (and our patrons are requesting them). We must continue to expand the idea of what a library can be, or we will fail to remain relevant for our communities.

The understanding, support, and buy-in from senior administrative staff are crucial to the success of projects launched with these new understandings of literacy and library service. At the same time, an organizational culture that values and supports innovation can be just as important. One of the biggest barriers to trying new ideas may be the fear around taking a risk and the possibility of failure. We believe that risk taking is essential for growth and innovation since taking risks and experiencing failure allow us to rethink, revise, and improve what we do.[1] An institutional tolerance for risk taking is perhaps the most critical prerequisite for undertaking projects like these.

TRADITIONAL BARRIERS

We have narrowed our focus to those barriers that are unique to technology-based programs. The one barrier that is noticeably absent is money. We believe, with some practical experience, that where there is a passion and a desire to do something, the resources can be found. There may be hard choices involved, the end product may not be exactly what was envisioned, but the change you want to make or the outcome that you're looking for can be achieved. Money can always be brought up as a barrier to innovation (and often is). If your organization truly doesn't want to move in a new direction or adopt a program, it is most valuable to understand the real reasons why.

Anyone who has worked for a length of time in an organization of any size has most likely run into roadblocks to developing new projects. In our experience there is usually a solution. And although the solution might change aspects of the project, a willingness to approach a new project as a work in progress will let you focus on the outcome you are planning for, rather than simply planning to avoid potential pitfalls. The common barriers we identified in our project are summarized in the following paragraphs.

COMMUNICATION AND MARKETING

Public libraries use a range of tools to alert patrons to upcoming programs and events. These include online calendars or event listings, flyers distributed in libraries and in community agencies, posters, and monthly or even quarterly publications. Libraries are likely to require events to be planned up to three to six months in advance so that announcements can be printed in paper publications. Although printed publications have a role to play in marketing programs, this kind of advance deadline doesn't allow for programming to be developed in response to more immediate interests, particularly of youth. This is one of the barriers to creating responsive and topical programs that are appealing to youth. An easy solution to this is to acknowledge that print publications that advertise a wide range of events for a long period of time are not the most effective way to reach youth. Producing smaller quantities of flyers and posters will let kids know what's happening and make program planning more responsive.

Most youth find out about our workshops from the library's website, friends, library staff, or posters. In addition, older youth tend not to plan ahead but visit the library in an opportunistic way —when it's convenient. We've found success in establishing a regular and consistent day of the week when one of a number of activities that appeal to youth can occur. This parallels our more traditional experience in libraries with story times—offer the same type of program on a the same day each week and you'll build an audience.

STAFF TIME AND SKILL

There are several major barriers around the issue of staffing technology programs. In an ideal world, any staff that is interested and has the skills can develop and run a program. But the world is not ideal. One issue to implementing programs is the question of what level of staff will be able to plan and conduct programs. In some libraries, only professional librarians are permitted to do these activities. In others, paraprofessional staff is able to carry out but not plan or manage programs and budgets. And in still others, any staff with an interest and the skills can plan and carry out programs. Each library is different: union or work rules may impact what's possible, as will historical practice. Of course, the simple availability of staff can be the key factor in this decision. If you're interested in pursuing technology programming but lack professional staff with the time or expertise to carry it out, look to engage and support those staff who delight in working with youth to develop and implement programs.

Once you have identified interested and available staff, the next issue is training. This is a two-part issue: first, who can do the training if it requires more than self-teaching; and second, how much training is required. Library staff tend to be motivated self-starters who can quickly grasp new concepts, so setting aside some uninterrupted time for focused study may be sufficient. Making contact with people outside the library is another excellent choice. There may be K–12 teachers in your local school district who can help out with programs that feature software tools. And, of course, there may be an online community of practitioners to work with.

In terms of how much training is enough, our experiences demonstrate that teacher-librarians don't need to know everything. They just need to be a bit ahead of their students and accept that they will often be learning right along with them. Co-learning has been proven effective, and it is a great way to establish trusting relationships with the kids.

ONE SIZE DOESN'T FIT ALL

The current structure of the organization, the available resources, and the cost of implementation–both direct and indirect—in developing technology programming for youth in public libraries are important considerations. There's no one-size-fits-all design. Technology programs have the potential to put pressure on scarce resources. They require the use of technology, which usually means a redistribution of existing tools or the acquisition of new ones—which are rarely free.[2] A library may have only one computer lab and a limited number of hours that it can be used. Using it for one purpose will mean something else doesn't happen. And unlike a children's story hour room, which has a single purpose, a computer lab is prime real estate for the full range of library patrons. Yet technology programs, like all library programs, need to start from the premise that if a program is worth doing, it is worth investing in thoughtfully and, if successful, worth doing again. By sharing our experiences with Media MashUp, we hope to highlight some of the challenges you may face once you decide technology programming is worth doing and to present solutions to help you go forward with workshops and classes for youth.

MEDIA MASHUP

THE BACK STORY

Back in 2006, we began our collaboration by bringing existing technology-based classes, workshops, and staff from the Learning Technologies Center (LTC) of the Science Museum of Minnesota (SMM) to the newly opened downtown branch of the Minneapolis Public Library (now Minneapolis Central, part of the Hennepin County Library System). We immediately discovered that we needed to deal thoughtfully with the information technology (IT) environment and staff. To do the kind of rich media programming that we wanted to introduce, we needed to have greater access to install software in public access computer labs than was typically provided to outside organizations. The computers that were available (desktops in a lab and a set of laptops) had standard images.

An image is a working profile of the computer with all settings and software applications tested and saved in a working state. Public access computers in many libraries have a standard image, or set of software, that is always available. Many libraries also have multiple images, which allow certain computers to make available specific pieces of software. For example, the Hennepin County Library has ten computer images that include a teen image, which has software supporting teen interests and homework needs, and a computer lab image, which includes the Microsoft Office(R) suite. Using standard images is a technique for managing software licenses throughout a large system where the cost of outfitting all computers with expensive software would be prohibitive. Software that is standard on an image is routinely tested and updated by the IT department.

At Minneapolis Central, the software image included Deep Freeze, a software that completely erased the computer between users, then reset all of the software applications. Deep Freeze enabled library patrons to download anything to the computer while they were using it, but it prevented them from making permanent changes to workstations that would interfere with the network's integrity or the activities of future users.

Any time that a computer was shut down, all projects and files in use and saved on the computer by the kids would be erased permanently. So it became obvious that each class we offered might end up being a one-time workshop. Based on the way the LTC normally delivered technology programs, we had planned to hold multiple-session classes and expected that kids would be able to save their work between sessions. It became apparent quickly (and sometimes painfully when we lost student work) that we couldn't do this. We needed to figure out how to install specific software to support our multiple-session classes, and we had to develop strategies that enabled participants to save their work between sessions.

Scratch, the software we chose, is a free, rich media content creation software that was in development in 2006 by the Lifelong Kindergarten group at the Massachusetts Institute of Technology (MIT) Media Lab. It was developed with National Science Foundation support specifically for use in after-school settings by youth. It is software that allows you to easily create rich media projects. The Scratch environment allows users to bring digital images, sounds, and music all together and save these as an interactive presentation.

We chose Scratch for several reasons, cost being only one factor. Our first workshops were held quite early in the development of Scratch. The LTC had an existing relationship with the Media Lab through the Lifelong Kindergarten group. It was an early test bed for Scratch and had already developed some successful workshops integrating the software. At that time Scratch was limited in that it allowed you to save files only to the computer itself. (The current version allows users to publish, or share, projects on an online website; our early testing helped developers understand the need to create this function for later versions.)

Without the option to share, we had to solve the problem of computers erasing everything when shut down, figure out how to offer multiple-session classes, and find a way to save participants' projects from one session to the next on the library's computers.

LTC staff work regularly with K–12 classroom teachers and the school's information technology (IT) support personnel. That experience, and an understanding that an IT staff's first responsibility is to ensure safe and secure systems in the library, convinced us to take preemptive action and set up a meeting early on to talk to the library's IT personnel about installing Scratch on the library's image. We knew we needed to speak from direct experience. Our aim was to establish trust, so we came to that first meeting with copies of Scratch installed on flash drives and CDs for the staff to try out and test. If we were able to speak to IT staff as peers (i.e., we knew what were talking about in the IT domain) and gain respect early on, we would have a better chance of creating a positive relationship with the people maintaining the software and hardware critical to the success of our workshops and classes. With the experiences we brought into the meetings as museum professionals, we understood the need for trust, and we acknowledged that we knew IT staff needed to understand the applications we wanted to use from their own perspective.

We had our meeting and shared LTCs experience with Scratch—that it was stable and did not have security issues. But, we assured the IT staff, we did not assume that they would be able to make a decision on installation and support until they had worked with and tested the programming application themselves. During our first meeting we gave a short demonstration of Scratch. We explained that because the program was in early development at the MIT Media Lab, we were able to share copies of the software with them, but we asked them not to share with others. We think that offering this access and connecting the software to a trusted institution gave us the credibility to have the IT staff consider our request. They really appreciated being brought in early and with full disclosure.

We treated IT staff as partners—to establish mutual respect, to collaborate with them on figuring out what we needed to do, and to answer their specific needs. Their questions focused on a few things: Was this new software a network security risk? Would it cause stability problems or any issues on the computers that it would be used on? We shared our experience from previous use in programs at the Science Museum of Minnesota and in schools that had tested the software. We had been using the software for about eight months in LTC labs without issue—for the network or for the computers used by youth—so we could share practical working experience. Working in schools had given us experience inside network systems that we did not control, with no ill effect or consequence for the school's network performance or integrity.

Because we started with such a sensitive approach to the IT staff's needs and concerns, they were happy to support us in implementing our workshops and classes. We got the green light, and the current version of the software was installed on computers that we would use. This didn't solve the problem of how and where we needed to save the projects, but we had support to get started and felt we would find a way to solve that problem.

Since we were piloting a new kind of technology class with a new kind of technology tool—directly from educational technology researchers—we needed to come up with solutions as we developed our workshop structure. We solved the problem by purchasing flash memory jump drives and saving all of the files youth created onto these at the end of each class. Along with this approach the LTC had also started prototyping and testing online services that would let us save directly from the computers to a web server at the Science Museum. This was part of LTC's work with the Media Lab that prototyped and tested an early version of a Scratch server platform. These early efforts were not automated—the instructor had to guide the workshop participants through a series of steps to save their projects—so the process was not foolproof.

The major issue related to saving youth projects was making sure we were able to catch them before they shut down the computers when they were finished so we could save their projects. What we learned as we actually started running classes was that we had to have strategies from within the context of the class to save the participant's projects. We also found that youth often didn't come back for multiple-session classes, even though the program plan was to have two- or three-session classes and they had signed up in advance.[3] Despite this, we still wanted to make sure we saved the projects because some youth *would* return and we couldn't predict who would and who wouldn't. These early experiences helped us improve the classes and gave us the impetus to create new workshops that addressed the needs of kids who attended only one session. Saving the projects also gave us a way to demonstrate how program participants were actually creating rich media in a drop-in setting at the library—for funders of our programs, for our research partners at MIT (who used this feedback for improving Scratch), and for developing our approach to technology programming in public libraries.

Through trial and error, then, we found several solutions to the initial issue of working with IT staff to get the software installed. There are additional barriers to adopting new programs, but they are not unique to those grounded in technology—how to get the right equipment (and enough of it) and how to negotiate for space in busy buildings. When we began Media MashUp, we were poised to work with our partner libraries to address the needs of their IT departments in implementing this approach.

FAST-FORWARD TO SOLUTIONS

We problem-solved and conceived of different solutions to ensure that staff in each of our Media MashUp libraries had access to the tools they needed. All of the software applications we selected are available at no cost, so the issue was not the cost of software. The workshops did not require the use of specialized hardware other than computers, though several libraries decided to use grant funds to purchase additional peripheral equipment such as PICO sensor boards or digital cameras.[4] At half of the libraries Scratch was already installed or installed quite readily by IT staff. In these libraries public services staff had gone through a process with IT to implement the software for previous programs. In one of these cases, a small library, one of the staff conducting the workshops was also the webmaster, which made the decision-making process straightforward.

One library was able to have all of the software applications installed on its public access image—but only for the duration of the Media MashUp programs and only at one library location. This was great, but the larger issue here was that after the grant-supported workshops had finished their scheduled run, the rich media applications were removed, even though the patrons who participated in the program may have wanted to continue working with the new software. In that case, the burden was on the patrons to come up with another avenue for accessing the software they had just been introduced to. While helpful for the project, this approach was less helpful for creating a consistent environment within the library to support rich media content creation. We were left wondering what would happen to the kids who enjoyed working with Scratch but lacked access to computers from home.

One of the libraries reduced barriers from an IT perspective because staff accepted full responsibility for all aspects of the technology (hardware and software) that was used in their workshops and classes. In this case, public services staff not only obtained the computers (using grant funds) but installed the software and provided technical support during their workshops. These same staff were ultimately responsible for replacing any equipment that might become damaged or nonfunctional. This is a creative way to work with IT, but it means that you need to have excellent support from managers because it goes against the grain to have staff other than IT staff be responsible for computer and software installation.

One of the libraries in our project actually had the need and, fortunately, enough latitude, to be able to create its own hardware and software platform for workshops and classes. The staff recycled donated laptop computers and installed a whole software operating system as well as all of the applications they needed to use for Media MashUp. To keep the cost low, they installed a version of Linux called Ubuntu. Linux is a free, open source operating system, and the Linux version of the software applications for Media MashUp was required. The success of this approach lay in the willingness of all parties to take a risk by giving up control. It also required substantial buy-in from all administrative staff.

The Learning Technologies Center prototyped this approach, which gives us a way to support our partners with hardware that might become available through recycling programs or gifts. In this particular case, the issue will be ongoing technical support. Technology programs that get their support from passionate individuals with specialized knowledge of these types of hardware and software systems, rather than from the library's investment in the program effort, may be on precarious ground.

If you lose access to the staff that has the passion and knowledge to support these initial efforts ,you lose the capacity for sustainability. On the other hand, this can open up opportunities for creative partnerships with local businesses and volunteer groups that may be able to donate equipment, energy, expertise, and time. This may hold the most promising direction, given the variety of constraints on public libraries that are funded from increasingly scarce government funds. This approach can bring together community organizations and the library systems to encourage patrons to develop 21st century skills, and it can support the evolving identity of public libraries as agencies for informal learning.

FINAL THOUGHTS

Libraries differ in their openness to technology. We know that the IT departments in some libraries fall under the jurisdiction of a larger entity (county or city government) that sets up additional hurdles for implementing technology programs. There may be requirements related to what kind of hardware can be purchased, regardless of the funding source. The solutions we discuss are ones we've seen work and are not meant to be exhaustive.

We know that having a robust set of strategies is important in working with IT staff who may not be comfortable with adding new computer applications to the library's computer images. We know, too, that software application selection is often a team-based process, so having a clear and direct way to communicate about the desired outcomes of technology programs to a diverse audience is important. We also believe in a variation of the adage that if something is worth doing it is worth doing well. Our version? If something is worth doing, it is worth doing, and working through the issues while implementing the program is part of the process.

If you aren't able to work with IT staff to have your software installed on the image, there are other ways to go. One solution is to use only software that can be run completely through a web browser. In that case, IT staff is generally less concerned; the software is not resident on the image, and there is no need for internal updating or management of licenses. There may be concerns about bandwidth use, but these are few, in part because other types of Internet use (streaming music or video, for example) are a much larger drain on capacity. The challenges are identifying software that will let you run the kind of workshops you'd like and finding a mechanism for saving projects created by participants.

Another reasonable solution is to use USB flash drives. We have found that these can be used effectively to bypass the need to put software applications (the actual programs) on library images. You can load the program software on a portable flash drive and use the drive to get participants access to the software. The software is simply run from the flash drive. It will take some experimentation and planning to make sure that the software applications you want to use will fit on a flash drive and be stable when run on the host computers, but a strong advantage of this approach is that you can use any available computers for your workshops and classes and work with other organizations to reach kids with technology-based workshops. Developing flash drives with the program software might be a great project for interns or volunteers.

For example, the applications that we use with Media MashUp can be installed and run from a flash drive. They include Scratch; a sound editing program called Audacity (http://audacity.sourceforge.net); Picasa (http://picasa.google.com), an image editing program; and ArtRage 2 Starter Edition (www.artrage.com/artrage-demos.html), a natural media drawing program. In chapter 7 we have a list of other free or low-cost software (with URLs) you might want to consider using in your technology workshops.

If you use flash drives as your way to provide access to the software, keep in mind that each piece of software must be fully installed; don't just copy the installer or the compressed (zipped) files. With a large enough flash drive you can even install both Windows- and

Macintosh-compatible versions of the software, which means you can truly take your workshops anywhere. Using flash drives for software access is the most flexible of the solutions, but means that the software applications you use can't be subject to copyright or licensing restrictions.

Another way to prepare a flash drive is to install programs on it called portable apps; however, a very specific preparation of applications on the flash drive has to be done before the software can be run. These portable applications on flash drives work only on computers that use a Windows operating system. Portable apps flash drives work well, and they're configured to easily save to the flash drive. Each flash drive can be assigned to a particular participant (or set of participants) so that people can find their work on that flash drive the next time they attend class.

The software programs we have used can also be run from a CD-ROM. CDs are inexpensive to purchase, and you can give the CD to a workshop participant if your budget allows. There are difficulties in using CDs, however. While library computers may have CD drives, they may lack the required software to burn to disks. CDs are also fragile and often will become damaged with wear and prone to failure during a workshop. Also—thinking ahead—CD-ROMs may be phased out as a distribution medium and many libraries are taking a thin-client approach to computing that removes bulky desktops, so they may not be the best solution in the future.

So there are some relatively straightforward solutions if you aren't able to add software to your library's image. A common concern among IT staff is related to network security and fidelity. There may be a concern that the software will open a hole in the secure network or, even worse, be malicious and destroy sensitive data. One solution we've alluded to is to use laptops and a public wireless network rather than desktop computers that are plugged directly into the library's network.

Image management on laptops can be done with DVDs. The DVD image contains a copy of all the desired software, and library patrons can download and use any software on the computer because it isn't connected to the secure network. When it is necessary to update the software applications, a centralized IT department can simply distribute a DVD with instructions for easy installation that any staff member can follow. This distributes the image management process across a wider range of staff, easing the burden on one department. Having the boot DVD available on-site also allows library staff to correct any issues that arise from allowing patrons to download directly from the Internet.

Finally, the development groups that are creating some of these software applications are starting to build versions of the applications that can run from within a web browser so that the application is not downloaded or installed on a computer. The drawback of using these versions of the applications is that they depend fully on access to the Internet. In some locations insufficient Internet bandwidth or high demand may create problems: the work may be slowed considerably while waiting for a response to commands sent. On the other hand, with the growth in smartphones and other handheld devices, this may be a promising approach. Imagine how many more kids you could serve if some bring their own devices.

Considering the potential for this direction we will want to be sensitive to how project work can be saved both for the workshop participants, who will want to have access to their work in the future, and for those who are running the program, so that they can support participants who return and need access to the workshop's artifacts to build upon for the future. This is a powerful solution to concerns about desktop and network security because the applications that run from the browser are already designed to limit access to the computer's operating system and hardware. This approach does bring up issues for workshops that use peripherals such as sensor boards and even webcams, which often need software support that browser-based applications may not provide.

So even if you can find ways to work more independently in establishing technology programs, you'll still want to maintain a strong working relationship with your IT department. They can become excellent allies, helping you to identify new tools and solutions in your quest to provide opportunities for youth to engage in rich media content creation and develop 21st century skills.

NOTES

1. YALSA, "Risky Business," Virtual President's Panel, 2010, www.yalsa.ala.org/yalsapresident2010/?page_id=9.
2. Molly Phipps, Organizational Change Interviews, 2009, www.hclib.org/extranet/MediaMashup/MediaMashUp_OrgChg0409.pdf.
3. In a later project we learned that our experience wasn't unique. Matt Gullett reported similar experiences in his work with the King County Library System. Discussion with the authors, April 13, 2010, Seattle, WA.
4. PICO boards are sensor boards created by the Scratch team that can be programmed using Scratch to respond to changes in the real world.

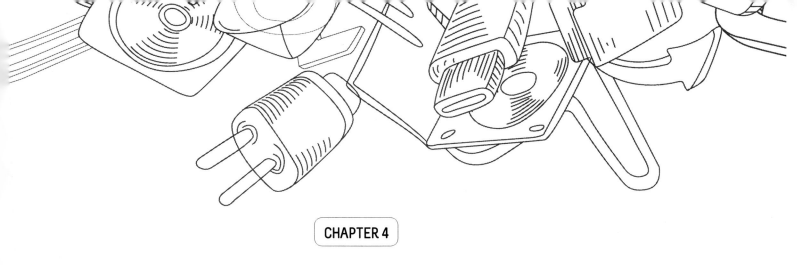

CHAPTER 4

Technology Programming for Youth

There are several approaches to developing technology programs that can be successful, depending on how your library organizes its youth programming. Many libraries take a seasonal approach to programming—offering activities for youth during fall, winter, spring, and summer. With funding constraints, some libraries focus on youth programming efforts more deeply in the summer or during out-of-school periods—Saturdays and holiday breaks. Others offer weekly workshops year-round. Any of these can be successful, and many libraries use a combination.

How libraries select and schedule programs is based on many factors. Room and equipment availability are critical factors that will determine how frequently you can offer technology programs. In many locations equipment and rooms are booked far in advance, or booking opens for only a limited time. You can also plan to take the programs out of your building to other organizations that serve school-age youth—your local YMCA or YWCA are great possible outreach sites. Some libraries have had success in developing programs that can be offered by any staff and on demand for groups that visit the library.

This chapter will give you a set of thoughtful questions to ask when you are considering offering technology-based programming for youth in your library. While our focus is on Scratch, we will also give you tips for identifying and working with your library's existing resources. We will guide you through the necessary preparations that will enhance your ability to offer successful technology-infused programming for youth at your library.

Although we hope to give you the kind of help that will prepare you for using other software tools in a workshop, we focus on Scratch because we have found it to be the most flexible and scalable by a range of staff. Other technology-based programs (one that focuses on using the commercial application Flash, for example) will require a greater depth of knowledge and learning by staff in order to successfully lead workshops, as well as a higher level of funding to support learners.

We'll also talk about how to prepare the learning space in your library and select equipment to ensure the success of your program. Your library may decide to hire other organizations to conduct workshops as it determines how best to offer technology-rich experiences for youth. In our experience there is no single approach, but rather a set of strategies for taking the best advantage of available resources. This chapter will be helpful in those situations as well. So let's look at what you'll need to do to define your audience, select staff, and prepare staff to teach.

A note on how we use specific terms. We use the word *program* to refer to an overarching approach to using technology in libraries. A technology-based program may include workshops, classes, activities, or demonstrations. We use the word *workshop* to refer to a one-session (regardless of whether it is one hour or three) technology creation experience and typically one project goal. We use the word *class* to refer to a multiple-session learning experience where there are multiple project goals.

PLANNING MATTERS

Planning begins with a core set of goals. The resources you will need for your workshop are defined by your goals—and depend a bit on how you approach developing the program and what outcomes you are looking for. Some programs may be developed around what's readily available; some come from good experiences in earlier programs, or as part of grant proposals. Others may begin with volunteers who bring in specific skills and expertise and a desire to help out the library.

While using a formal logic model or outcomes-based approach is always a good idea, you can start off with a few key things in mind. There's nothing wrong with going back later and doing more formal planning. First, you must be able to articulate for yourself first and then for others why you want to offer the workshop and how you will position it as part of a broader strategic effort to reach youth in your community. Next, you need to know what resources are available to do what you want to do in terms of space, staff, equipment, software, and money . . . and whatever else you need to go forward. Last, you need a clear understanding of your intended audience and how the program will serve its needs in the short term.

SETTING GOALS

At its heart, each Scratch workshop is a design-based workshop. Its purpose is to teach design thinking in a programmable media environment (Scratch) that allows participants to develop a project in a relatively short period of time.

In planning your workshop you will want to set two kinds of goals—those for the kids who attend the program and those for yourself. It's comparatively easy to set goals for kids. You may want them to experience the library as a safe place or develop a particular skill (we'll talk more about outcomes for youth later), but setting goals for yourself and determining what you want to achieve with the workshop is equally important. As you consider the outcomes for yourself, think about the range of reasons why you provide programs for youth in general, what gives you satisfaction in working with kids, and what personal and professional skills you'd like to advance by teaching this, or any other, workshop. In short, what is your passion around serving youth through programs and how do you harness it?

Successful programs are built on the passions of the instructors and the participants. Passion can be related to addressing the needs of youth in your community around technology, about providing safe space for youth during out-of-school time, or about the library's role in leveling the playing field for disadvantaged kids in your neighborhood. It may be about promoting work around the community of Scratch itself. Being able to identify where the passion lives is key to creating a successful program. But assuring success in technology programs is particularly important because you will need to "sell" the program to administrators or IT department staff. And a key to this is being able to advocate articulately and passionately for your youth.

We offer a few possible goals you might consider as your reason for offering technology workshops for kids. You will discover others in your own library and community and you can even have kids help you design meaningful ones.

- You may want to use this workshop as one way *to create a supportive atmosphere around learning and engagement in your library.* Using the workshops to create this atmosphere makes the library a more trusted and relevant place that youth will want to return to for other programs, or help with homework, or to sample the other out-of-school-time activities that you offer.
- You might offer the workshops because you want *to learn more about how kids learn* so that you can better respond to their needs in other programs you develop.
- You may want to see if *kids can work cooperatively in your environment—* for example, to see how another activity, like a book club, may be better

structured to support their interests and thus support positive youth development.

- You may want to offer it as a way *to bring more girls (or boys) into the library*.
- You may need *to use lab space or equipment for a certain number of hours per week*, or risk losing it.
- You may even want to use a workshop as a way *to develop a gallery of Scratch projects from your library for the world to see* on the Scratch website to promote your programs.

Short-term outcomes for youth workshop participants can be related to specific technology skills, to behaviors (in the library or outside), or to literacy skills, in particular those identified as 21st century.

Designing programs with desired outcomes in mind will help you market your programs effectively to a wide range of potential participants and potential financial supporters. It also provides a good mechanism for developing tools for evaluating and measuring the success of programs. This is a shift for many libraries, which traditionally have focused on measuring success by numbers—for example the number of people attending an author reading or checking out a book. While counting the numbers is important, it may be more valuable in today's climate of scarce resources to be able to articulate the meaning of the programs that we offer.

A great way to approach program planning is to develop a range of desired outcomes that touch on key areas, and to acknowledge from the start that not every child will achieve each outcome. Specific outcomes for Scratch-based programs include developing 21st century literacy skills—leadership, problem solving, creativity, and innovation. Keep in mind, though, that we can't control what kids actually get from our programs. We can, however, take comfort in knowing that if we plan thoughtfully, allow for a range of possible outcomes, and focus on quality, participants will, at a minimum, experience the library as a safe and welcoming environment.

ONE APPROACH TO MEASURING OUTCOMES

We use a very simple evaluation approach with short-term outcomes for Scratch workshops. We set up a short online survey on SurveyMonkey for the kids to fill out. (Questions are provided in table 4.1.) Some libraries print the survey, have the kids fill out a paper version, and then enlist a volunteer to enter responses into the online version. This may make it easier to manage workflow and get the kids to complete the survey. It also alleviates the potential problem of lack of Internet access and ensures that kids fill them out. We always keep in mind that we don't necessarily have kids for more than one session, so we can't easily track change over time the way many evaluations do.

Because of this, the evaluation needs to focus on what participants experience in a particular session—the immediate outcome. Although it may be less satisfying to talk about short-term outcomes than long-term ones, these are important as well. If the workshop has the short-term outcome of a focused and settled group of kids for two hours, this is a good thing for all library users and creates a positive climate in our busy buildings. The other facet to consider when thinking about outcomes is how they are measured. We've found that participant surveys tell one story, but reflections from workshop leaders tell an equally important story. And building in the opportunity for staff to have a few minutes for reflection is important.

Here are the questions we asked youth about their Scratch experience paired with what we were hoping to measure and what we learned. We also asked about workshop locations, but that question isn't repeated here.

Based on the responses, we made changes in how we offered the workshops the next time. For example, we set up the room so that kids work at tables of two. We became more

Table 4.1

WORKSHOP EVALUATION

WHAT WE ASKED:	WHY WE ASKED:	WHAT WE LEARNED:
Did you save a project to the Scratch website today?	to see if kids were able to get to the Scratch website	Most of the time they were able to get there, but they didn't always like their project enough to post.
Did you learn something new today?	to see if the kids were aware they learned something	With both newcomers and established users, we were less interested in whether they learned the specific project than whether they learned something new. More than 90 percent of the kids learned something new, often things we didn't expect, but frequently related to what we wanted them to learn.
How did you work on your project today? (alone, with others, with the instructor)	to learn if kids collaborated —a key 21st century skill	Fifth and sixth graders were less interested in working together and learned more from the instructor.
Of all that you did today, what are you most proud of?	to give the kids a chance to champion themselves.	Some kids prized their technique with Scratch, some their ability to help others, and some everything they did.

deliberate about teaching by having the kids "ask three before me"—telling them at the beginning that if they are stuck they should first ask their neighbor for help, then another participant, then check the help tools in Scratch before finally asking the instructor. This fosters a climate of co-learning. It gets kids to work together more comfortably and builds leadership capacity among the participants. Once the instructor has identified kids who are comfortable in this role, he or she can enlist them, informally, to help teach others. Co-learning develops loyal repeat participants because kids with greater technical skill know there is a place for them in the workshop.

CHILDREN'S DEVELOPMENTAL STAGES

When planning a workshop, it's important to grasp the developmental stage of the kids you're trying to reach. Not understanding their needs and interests will keep you from having a successful workshop and may cause your participants to become restless or unfocused. We all know that any given child will display developmental characteristics that are both above and below what we know as typical. Knowing ahead of time that there will be a disparity in needs and abilities helps you plan a workshop that will reach kids with multiple abilities, interests, and inclinations.

A quick review of Piaget's work provides a common ground for understanding children's developmental stages and how they learn. Piaget's research strongly supports the need for active engagement in the environment—hands-on learning. Knowledge of the cognitive development process helps us understand how to teach and structure our workshops and how to develop better relationships with youth. Scratch uses a constructionist learning perspective with foundations in Piaget's work, so if you have chosen to use Scratch, you are already moving in the right direction.

It's beyond the scope of this book to do a full review of cognitive development, but it is important to touch on its premises. Piaget described kids ages seven to twelve as *concrete operational*. The key characteristics of children of this age are an interest in sequence and patterns, a decentering approach to problem solving, and growing skills in classification. The relevant observation is that kids in this stage can "only solve problems that apply to actual (concrete) objects or events, not abstract concepts or hypothetical tasks."[1] Starting at about age eleven, kids enter the *formal operational* stage. Kids at this age begin to use trial and error for problem solving, so older children will be well suited to projects that engage these higher-order skills.[2] Interested readers will find resources for in-depth discussion and exploration on these topics at the end of the book

Knowing about yourself as a learner—the way we teach tends to reflect our traits as learners—is also important. And at this point in your life there may not be the opportunity for you to radically change how you learn, but your awareness of how you behave as a learner will let you design your workshop, taking into account your natural strengths and biases. Most librarians learn through interaction with text. Books, reading, and the written word are our primary paths to knowledge. This is in deep contrast with today's youth, who are kinesthetic, visual, and experiential learners; they learn by touching, looking, and doing.

You will be most successful and create the best experience by setting realistic expectations for the youth attending your workshops. Plan for a range of attention spans, provide space that is conducive to movement as well as stationary work, and, most of all, get to know your youths' interests and needs, both educational and social. This kind of preparation and research will ensure that the environment, the time, the hardware and software, and the materials you use will meet the needs of your audience.

While Scratch offers itself as a technology tool with wide applicability for kids ages eight and up, the age of the participants is a factor in designing an effective workshop. Each age and stage of childhood offers a different opportunity for youth to interact with software and media, creation and exploration. In other words, a program that works for 10- and 11-year-olds isn't necessarily going to work for thirteen- or fourteen-year-olds; sixteen- and seventeen-year-olds can be reached through affordable technology programming, but in a different way. We'll provide projects in the next chapters that address these realities, but for now, here are a couple of basic premises to provide a foundation for successful workshops for most children.

FOUNDATION FOR SUCCESS

Whether or not you use Scratch, the software application you select needs to support kids in multiple places—their intellectual world, their social world, and their physical world.

This approach, which supports multiple connections, allows the learner to engage more deeply. Scratch has been successful for our library programs because it manages to overlap these three worlds, as illustrated in figure 4.1. Thoughtful instructors can harness the natural energy of groups of kids by selecting a tool that gives them a chance to make purposeful connections between what they are thinking about, what they're talking about, and where they are.

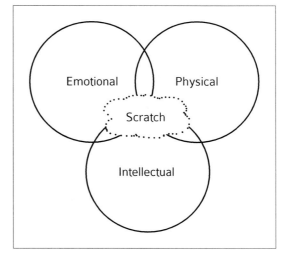

FIGURE 4.1   Scratch engages learners on many levels.

Children want to belong to a peer group as well as understand and even change their status in that group. Offering programs that have the flexibility to allow them to self-select as leaders is key, as is the willingness of the program instructor to step back to support kids' endeavors to become leaders and learners. The key to doing this successfully lies in understanding that a technology program needs to do more for kids than just teach them a technique or how to use a tool. It must provide relevance—show them why they want to use it and how it can enrich their lives. Workshops that teach kids how to record and edit audio using specialized software enables a child interested in music to explore those interests while building his or her skills in an environment that is free from any consequences for failure. Success needs to be measured by what an individual is able to explore and reflect on—not a fixed end product.

WORKSHOP MODELS

We have developed two distinct ways to use Scratch in public libraries that incorporate these ideas—formal workshops and open studios. While our focus is Scratch, these approaches can work for any technology-based programs.

FORMAL WORKSHOPS

Formal workshops have a distinct learning focus. They are often built around teaching the process of how to complete a particular type of project—creating an electronic greeting card or a simple game—or around using particular features of the software and its tools. There are specific learning goals—a starting point and an end point for participating youth and the teacher. Again, though, we don't consider a child has failed if he or she doesn't end the class with a fully completed project.

Formal workshops can be designed for all ages. A workshop for eight- to ten-year-olds who are inexperienced Scratch users, for example, will be most successful if it has a defined project outcome. This structural component meets the need of the age group for a concrete learning experience. The project outcome doesn't need to be complex. For older children who have some experience with Scratch, a formal workshop is a chance to fully develop a complex project—a game, for example. This meets the need of older youth to develop higher-level thinking and problem-solving skills.

OPEN STUDIOS

Open studios, which open the way to a wide range of possible questions, can be challenging for the instructor, though the challenges are not insurmountable. In fact, they offer an opportunity for engaging more experienced youth participants as co-teachers, which helps youth build collaboration and leadership skills. Open studios require the instructor to let go of being the expert who has all the answers, which, in turn, creates a wonderful opportunity for kids to teach one another and to solve problems independently using the wealth of Scratch resources to find answers. It is important how we, as adults, model the ongoing process of learning for our kids. We can let them see that no one has all the answers, but by working together we can find them.

Cynthia Matthias, a teen librarian at the Hennepin County Library with a lot of experience running both kinds of workshops, advises that although open studios need to be organized around a specific project or purpose, kids can still be encouraged to explore and follow their own paths as they create. Success with this approach is not that every kid ends up with the same product but that each participant experiences a personal or group learning experience. The open studio format allows youth who are motivated to complete projects to succeed and those who just like to tinker an opportunity to be just as successful. Open studios place different demands on the teacher than formal workshops do, but they don't force every child into the same mold, and they provide the added benefit of more opportunities for youth to challenge themselves.

Open studios can be successful for kids of any age as well as kids with some experience or none at all. It will be up to the instructor to decide when to offer which program based on the desired learning experience. Looking at the two models as a pathway and a cycle may help librarians develop ongoing programming for both new and experienced participants.

We developed open studios as loosely structured opportunities for kids to explore Scratch programming on their own, but with available guidance. Sometimes these programs included hardware beyond the computer—a sensor board that can be used to notice phenomena in the environment—light, sound, and motion, such as PICO boards or Lego WeDo—Scratch add-ons that let you control small motors. Digital cameras or drawing tablets are also possibilities. Or open studios may simply be a chance for novices and experienced users to spend time working on their own ideas to gain fluency with Scratch in a safe and supportive community.

A NOTE ON REAL-WORLD CONNECTIONS IN WORKSHOPS

Both formal workshops and open studios tend to be more successful if there are physical world components to the activities. Whenever possible, embed a direct link to the physical world in technology workshops. Modeling (in paper or with motors or sensors) what we want to do in the virtual world makes a project more concrete and deepens the learning experience. Real-world links also expand opportunities for youth who are kinesthetic or experiential learners.

LEARNING SPACES AND SCHEDULING

There are a couple of different approaches to finding space to hold your technology-based workshop. The good news is that there are few wrong places in which to hold a workshop. Keeping in mind your desired outcomes and goals, a number of situations can work.

In general, a space with at least three walls that includes wall space for a display screen (in other words, not all windows) is going to work best. This may be an area within your library that already has public access computers available or a space where you can bring in laptops. We've done some workshops on the public floor using public computers, but, in general, the demand on public access computers during open hours is so great that it's not worth pursuing. If, however, you can open early to allow the kids to come in, this can be successful. This approach works best if you are providing the workshop for a group of kids from an established organization such as a YMCA or school group. It will ensure that there will be adult leaders who can focus on keeping kids from wandering throughout the library while you focus on teaching.

Scheduling workshops in this manner may also help your library to be a more responsive partner with other out-of-school-time organizations. The willingness to adapt schedules to the needs of outside partners may have multiple benefits. Some library systems have branches that don't open until noon, and ones that close as early as five in the afternoon. When we are able to adjust staff schedules to permit "inreach" to our community partners, we reap benefits that go beyond the outcomes of any particular activity. We build the library as a multilayered resource for learning and literacy.

One idea that has succeeded on multiple fronts was implemented at the Hennepin County Library's Brooklyn Park location. The library, which has three elementary schools in its service area, typically closes at six on Thursdays. The library hosts an open house for each school once a semester—inviting the entire student body in for a two-hour event. The main purpose of the event is to establish the library as a resource for families of school-age kids. But in addition to library card sign-ups, Cynthia, the teen librarian, sets up laptop computers in the high-traffic area and gives minilessons on using Scratch to small groups of kids. With attendance at these events close to two hundred, she touches a wide range of kids with the technology program. The direct benefit was that those same kids later came back to the library for longer workshops.

Many libraries play a key role as a community gathering spot and a meeting room that supports workshops. Not all meeting rooms will be ideal for a technology workshop, however. We have seen meeting rooms with four glass walls, for example, or ones with inadequate wiring. For the moment, however, we'll take for granted that you are able to cobble together a few tables and extension cords. Depending on the intended age of the kids in your workshop and the number of volunteers, a number of setups can be successful.

If you have a desktop projector available, you can position the controls for it in the back of the room. Standing in the back of the room, the instructor can see what everyone is doing. This makes it easy to notice youth who may have questions or to see that they've moved on from what you are demonstrating. This is sometimes an issue with teens who visit Facebook or YouTube at regular intervals. Positioning the computer and projector toward the front of the room allows you to see how they may be feeling, which can be helpful for younger kids. If you are in a newer building, you may have a ceiling-mounted projector, which makes it easy to put the instructor's workstation anywhere in the room. As you run the workshop, keep in mind that the projector and screen are used only to demonstrate

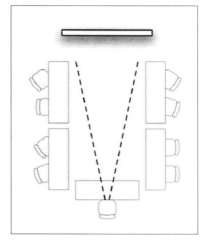

FIGURE 4.2   U-Shaped Table Arrangement

technique and show features of the project. You want an arrangement that lets you and your volunteers move freely about the room and enough space to stop behind kids to offer guidance and support.

You may not have control over how the tables and computers are set up. But if you do, we have found that a U-shaped arrangement of tables, shown in figure 4.2, works well for these purposes. The instructor's computer can be positioned in the opening; kids are able to work next to one another. You and any volunteers can easily walk behind the participants.

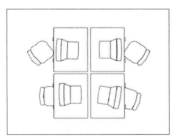

FIGURE 4.3   Square Table Arrangement

Arranging tables in a square, shown in figure 4.3, can work well for desktop computers.

If you are able to use laptop computers you'll have much more flexibility with room setup. The issue to consider with laptops is where outlets are located and how to ensure safety in the room by bundling and covering up power cords. You may also need power strips if the number of outlets in the room is insufficient or if they are situated on walls rather than in the floor. Again, your intimate knowledge of how the room is constructed will help you make the best decisions about how to arrange the room. You'll probably want to experiment to find what works best for you.

A MODEL WORTH CONSIDERING

Technology workshops in libraries will likely be in multipurpose rooms that will be reconfigured each time. If you are able to do some remodeling or planning for new space, the

Computer Clubhouse model is one that works well and is built to be dedicated all the time to youth working creatively with technology.[3] This model has elements you may be able to incorporate in existing spaces. One feature of the clubhouses worldwide, for example, is a green central table, used as a gathering and communal design space. Having a green table as a permanent fixture may not be possible in library spaces, but the concept of a gathering space can be replicated.

Your gathering spot can be marked by a sign or as a place for equipment that will be used in the day's session. You can also carve out space on the floor, near a whiteboard or flip chart where you can note kids' ideas and plans for the day. Using floor space to gather and talk about the day's activities works best with younger kids; older teens will likely want to have equipment nearby and be more comfortable in chairs around a table or in a circle.

Again, though, the space you have available may be limited and the idea is that you have a space where kids can learn to come for help or to get ideas. If you are fortunate enough to have permanent space available to build a rich media creation area, check out the Computer Clubhouse model or *Hanging Out, Messing Around and Geeking Out* for ideas.[4] The YOUmedia space at the Chicago Public Library was developed based on this research and provides an example of how such space can be configured in a way that maximizes the needs of teens around creation while preserving the security and multiple teaching modes appropriate for technology workshops in public libraries.

You will also want to make sure that the room you are using is appropriate for the activities you have planned. If photography requires darkness, can the room be completely darkened? Are the tables large enough to let kids spread out drawing materials? Are there enough outlets or power strips for multiple power cords? Can the door be shut if the kids get a little noisy? There will always be compromises in using existing space, but usually these can be successfully managed.

THE RIGHT STAFF

Are librarians teachers? Should they be? In some types of libraries (such as the school library media center) the answer is clearly yes. In other libraries (a corporate library, for instance) the answer is clearly no. And at the center of the continuum—public libraries—the answer isn't always clear. While librarians advance the acquisition of all types of knowledge, we aren't always comfortable as teachers standing in front of a group leading a lesson. Yet in the space between school and home, librarians can be quite successful.

First and foremost, a leader needs to demonstrate passion—about working directly with kids, about particular software or technology, or about one of the arts. The important thing is that the youth we serve can feel our enthusiasm, and they feed off it! Passionate teachers and learners, we've found, often use technology outside the context of work. In this respect, there's a key similarity between librarians who work with technology and those who are passionate about storytelling, who bring new books home to read on weekends. It's only the tools and techniques that differ. Like their storytelling counterparts, leaders of technology workshops need a keen understanding of children's developmental stages, appropriate expectations about what children can accomplish, and a willingness to foster an atmosphere for creative exploration and discovery.

As teachers, we must also be learners. We need to let others see our learning process and be willing to model that making mistakes is okay. Our experience shows that adopting a stance as a co-learner with youth allows us to gain their respect, particularly with older youth (twelve and up). This is not to say we have no leadership role. We are guides who create the setting for exploration and discovery. We set up an appropriate structure (the physical environment and the learning space for kids to be successful), then we move out of the way to let learning happen.

Teaching in this manner requires a unique set of skills and a willingness to tolerate a certain amount of unstructured activity (some might describe this as controlled chaos). Important learning is happening in a continuous cycle even if the kids don't come to a completed product at the end of a workshop. The learning that happens in the process of discovery is perhaps more important than simply finishing a project. This tolerance for seeing process as an end in itself is often difficult, yet it is a key facet of informal learning in libraries. We don't need to grade or measure kids on their finished products, which reduces the pressure to produce specific results.

Workshop leaders and teachers need to feel comfortable with the tool or material they are teaching. This doesn't mean a leader must know everything about it. Rather, it means knowing how to complete the project that is the focus of the workshop, knowing how to locate and use many kinds of help, and having an interest in building knowledge and skills with the hardware/software being used. In addition, the ability to troubleshoot well is a key skill. Trust that each time you teach a class you'll learn something new, which will help you prepare for the next time.

If you aren't comfortable with hardware, make sure to schedule your workshops when IT staff is available to step in if equipment issues come up. Always remember that you are cultivating a set of interested learners who can share their creativity and knowledge with you, whether they be youth participants, other librarians, or IT staff.

VOLUNTEERS

Volunteers are very helpful for the smooth operation of Scratch workshops. Adults and teens alike can make a valuable contribution if they possess the right attitudes, experience, and interest. However, as with any other volunteer experience, the more deeply you can engage each individual volunteer in developing and running the workshops and working with youth, the more reliable they will be. Like library staff, volunteers will also develop richer skills and techniques for using Scratch.

Volunteers can be engaged on a one-time or an ongoing basis, as fits your library's volunteer program. They can help teach skills and manage the kids in the room. Our approach to locating teachers and volunteers is to seek out those who approach teaching and learning as we do and are comfortable working with youth. But if people with excellent technical skills lack people skills to lead a workshop, there can still be a place for them. Let them work directly with you to help develop the workshop content and instruction guides rather than working with youth in the lab space. A really tech-savvy volunteer can help you train other volunteers as well.

Clearly, the key characteristics that volunteers need are similar to those needed by the staff. These characteristics include the ability to ask questions and help kids articulate what they are trying to accomplish—kind of like a reference interview. Volunteers should have experience working with the themes and creating the workshop project or at least be familiar with the software being used. They need to be light on their toes, able to move quickly between kids with different needs and skills. Patience is a crucial quality as is a genuine desire to work with kids.

Depending on your youth participants, you may want to consider bilingual volunteers who can help you teach children for whom English is not the first language. Scratch is unique in that it dynamically supports language translations in more than twenty-six languages. In an early workshop at the Minneapolis Public Library, Vicente, a Spanish-language library liaison translated for Keith, our English-speaking instructor, to teach a Scratch workshop for Latino kids. Keith knows Scratch well enough that he was able to change the screen display into Spanish for the ease of the kids. And we were delighted when midway through the workshop one young girl excitedly shared with the Spanish-speaking class that she was creating in Scratch using her native language—Portuguese! While at the Minneapolis library we were able to use paid staff, this workshop could have worked equally well with volunteers.

In the Hennepin County library system we've had volunteers as well as paid teen employees to help with Scratch workshops. We've found that the teens who work out the best are those who are interested in the social aspects of our programs—working with others—not those who are more technologically focused. Given how easy it is to learn Scratch, we are confident that most anyone can pick up the essential skills needed in order to help others in their learning.

Older teens can be extremely effective in working with the younger kids. Using youth as volunteers is a powerful experience for all involved. Younger kids benefit from working directly with older one who aren't siblings, and they tend to respond well to instruction and guidance. For teens who may not be successful in other settings, this is a tremendous benefit, and adults who work with youth volunteers benefit by learning more about youth culture. What's more, building such relationships helps to position the library as a community gathering space and creates a vibrant, multigenerational, informal learning community.

To mobilize teens as volunteers, contact your local high school. Many high schools now require community service as a graduation requirement. National Honor Society and International Baccalaureate programs have similar requirements that you can identify and tap into. These schools typically have a community liaison who can help students connect with your program. Robotics and art workshops offered by other local informal organizations are additional sources for volunteers. Don't hesitate to mention technology workshop volunteer opportunities to participants in your own existing teen groups. Book club or gaming program regulars are prime candidates.

You can pitch the opportunity to volunteer as a way to gain valuable job skills, to hone their technology skills, and to explore career options. You'll be helping them build those critical developmental assets in a win-win situation. They will have a chance to practice interview skills and get regular feedback as they grow their skills in a position of responsibility. Finally, after working with them, you can offer them a great letter of recommendation. Once you've been running technology programs for a couple of years, you'll probably have program participants who will be eager to help as volunteers as they get older. Sow the seeds for future volunteers by acknowledging the budding skills of younger kids in your workshops.

Local colleges and university teaching programs (or library schools) are also resources for volunteers, who will benefit from an opportunity to build relationships with your library and with youth in the community. Students in engineering or computer science programs may bring along a unique skill set. The Free Library of Philadelphia, which has strong partnerships with local colleges and universities, had a great success with this approach to Media MashUp. Interns spent the summer collaborating with library staff to develop specialized programs such as robotics. This was a great situation for all of participants. The college interns were able to work on creative projects with kids. The library was able to leverage highly skilled volunteers with no direct costs. And the kids got to make some really cool projects.[5]

Design professionals in your community can be great additions to your volunteer ranks because they bring a higher level of creative thinking with them. By developing strong partnerships with design professionals' organizations, you can continuously generate a pool of volunteers.

While there are few direct costs to hiring volunteers, managing them can be time consuming. Your library may have an established volunteer program that centrally manages volunteers. If not, take advantage of whoever in your library can help you with support tasks such as running background checks, holding orientation and training sessions, and interviewing. To take full advantage of what volunteers can do for you, you'll want to plan thoughtfully and be very explicit in the skills you are looking for, the training required, and the time commitment. Develop a job description that is aligned with these skills so that expectations are crystal clear. You will get out of your volunteers what you put into their training and support.

GROWING AUDIENCES

How you market and publicize your programs will depend on the age of the kids you are trying to reach, whether registration is required, and how your library approaches scheduling and marketing programs. It will also depend on whether you are offering a formal workshop or an open studio. Many libraries offer residents a periodic program brochure that lists all of the library's upcoming events and workshops for a two- to four-month time period. To be listed in a program brochure such as this typically requires that programs be planned up to six months ahead of time. Planning will need to be far enough along that a succinct and appealing description can be written. This limits your flexibility for the content of your workshop and the ability to be responsive to shorter-term interests of kids.

On the other hand, chances are that it is a parent who is reviewing the brochure, not the kid, so how you describe the program has to sound interesting enough for a parent to appreciate the content and its appeal to kids. But a parent may not have the technological or digital savvy to understand what digital or rich media content creation is. We've found it most helpful to have a stock title such as: Tech Creation Sandbox or Digital Design Workshop and a stock description such as: bring a friend and learn how to use new software to create digital projects. Remember, designing these marketing pieces is as much an art as it is a practical part of your job.

The most successful marketing strategy we've found for technology workshops is hand selling directly to youth by library staff. The direct approach is usually accompanied by a quarter-page flyer that gives the time, topic, and location with an appealing graphic. We often use graphics from projects that kids have created—giving full credit to the artist. Staff who encounter youth in the library, or in outreach visits to schools or other community agencies, give a personal invitation to kids, making sure to also say hello when the youth actually attend. Although this is time consuming, it does help with one of the ultimate goals of youth services, which is building relationships. If your library has an online calendar that allows you to post events for teens on a teen-directed page, this can be quite effective as well. Don't underestimate the power of a standard library poster as well. We use the same graphic and words as on the quarter-page flyer, which makes it easier to produce. We also use a template with an eye-catching banner to brand the programs with our color palette.

In order to effectively describe your program for any marketing and publicity pieces, you will need to develop the basics for the project, figure out how long it will take to move through each facet or section, and plan for contingencies. Contingencies can include every-thing from a need to cancel one session, to in-class equipment malfunctions, to having kids in each session with different skills. To plan effectively for contingencies, our best advice is to build flexibility within structure. The sample programs we describe in chapter 6 will show you how to accomplish this in a meaningful way.

OUTREACH

Once you've gained comfort with Scratch, learned how to set up your space, and run some workshops, you may want to think about how you can increase your audience at in-library programs or bring the programs you have done into the community. You can pitch the work-shops to existing partners, like the Seattle Public Library has done with the YMCA. Group leaders have brought kids in periodically to learn about Scratch, and Seattle staff returned the visits. Boy Scout and Girl Scouts troops in your area may also be interested in coming in to the library. If your library has an outreach program, you may be able to offer your Scratch programs in this way. Jason Hyatt at the Charlotte Mecklenburg Library has taken laptops from the library to the local juvenile correctional facility as part of ongoing programming for incarcerated youth. Not all partner organizations will have the necessary infrastructure for you to come in, and you may not have equipment to take out, but it is certainly worth exploring so that you can create programs that build your library's informal learning com-munity.

NOTES

1. "Piaget's Theory of Cognitive Development," *Wikipedia*, http://en.wikipedia.org/wiki/Theory_of _cognitive_development.
2. J. W. Santrock, *A Topical Approach to Life Span Development* (New York: McGraw-Hill, 2008).
3. Kylie Peppler et al. *The Computer Clubhouse: Constructionism and Creativity in Youth Communities* (New York: Teacher's College Press, 2009).
4. Mizuko Ito et al. *Hanging Out, Messing Around and Geeking Out* (Cambridge, MA: MIT Press, 2009).
5. Juan Suarez Romero, "Library Programming with LEGO MINDSTORMS, Scratch, and PicoCricket: Analysis of Best Practices for Public Libraries," *Computers in Libraries* 30, no. 1 (2010): 16–45.

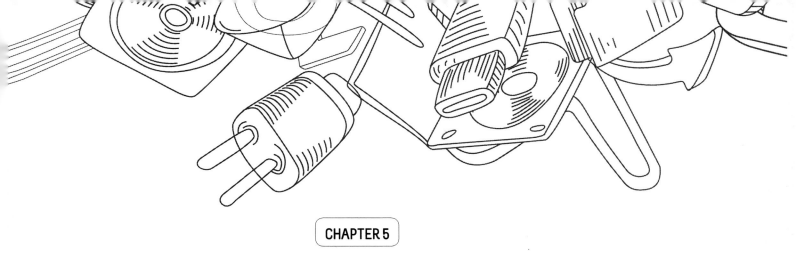

CHAPTER 5

Preparing for Workshops

We hope that you now have an idea how technology workshops can fit into youth programming at your library. You should also have a good understanding of the resources you'll need to support and run them. We'll focus in this chapter on Scratch and why it's a great choice for library-based workshops. We'll discuss an approach to teaching, present workshop formats, and take a look at the hardware and software that can support them.

WHY SCRATCH?

Scratch was designed to support learners' curiosity and creativity, their desire to design, create, experiment, and explore. Underlying Scratch is the belief that deep learning happens in cyclical movement through opportunities to imagine, create, play, share, and reflect.[1]

Mitchel Resnick, the director of the Lifelong Kindergarten Group at the MIT Media Lab, wrote this about Scratch: "People imagine what they want to do, create a project based on their ideas, play with their creations, share their ideas and creations with others, and reflect on their experiences—all of which leads them to imagine new ideas and new projects."[2]

Scratch is an example of interactive rich media content creation software. This is a bit of a mouthful, but what it essentially means is that you can build Scratch projects incorporating a range of digital media within the software framework. Scratch was designed to have

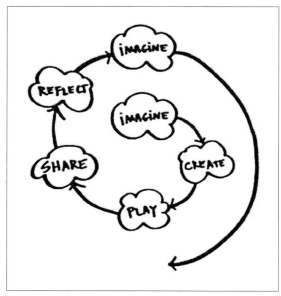

FIGURE 5.1   Elements of Deep Learning

a low floor (it's easily learned), a high ceiling (complex projects can be created in it), and wide walls (projects can incorporate a variety of digital content created outside of it).[3] Music, drawings, and digital photographs, for example, can be incorporated in games, animations, and music videos made in Scratch. Interactive projects can be built that require input from the user or player. It was intentionally designed to be flexible and to support the learner's personal interests, and because it allows so many different kinds of projects to be built, it can capture the interest of just about anyone. The opportunities Scratch offers are equally attractive to both boys and girls, and the software is as easy to use for storytelling and narrative exposition as it is for making video games and simulations. For example, a quick search on the Scratch site (http://scratch .mit.edu) reveals thousands of projects tagged as stories: stories written with virtual pages that can be turned, reviews of traditional print books (try searching for the popular Harry Potter or Twilight series), magazines, and even how-to manuals for using Scratch itself! The social networking features of the website let creators post their projects, receive comments, and carry on conversations with other Scratchers, and the interactive projects posted on the website are played by thousands of site visitors.

What makes Scratch so valuable is that it does all of this while also teaching basic computer programming skills. Created specifically for informal learning settings, it is a very thoughtful program for teaching design on the one hand and computer programming skills on the other, making it a powerful platform for playful learning, exploration, and discovery.

SCRATCH AND LIBRARIES

From the most practical perspective, Scratch is a very good match for public libraries because it is a free and tested application. It's also of great value to patrons because it opens the way to opportunities that extend beyond a library visit to home, school, or other locations. Created by the Lifelong Kindergarten Group and developed with support from the National Science Foundation (NSF #0325828), Scratch is part of a continuing series of programming software tools designed specifically for kids. It had its genesis in computer programming language environments such as Seymour Papert's groundbreaking Logo and Alan Kay's Squeak and Etoys

Scratch was developed to take advantage of the Internet and technologies such as highly graphical computer interfaces, but its developers have expertise in child development as well as computer programming. Information about the developmental learning stages of children gives Scratch a solid grounding in literacy skill development to combine with advances in the software and hardware that support approaches to computer programming literacy. The result is software that incorporates new understandings of what kids need to learn today and how they can learn it.

TEACHING SCRATCH: A JUST-IN-TIME MODEL

Through years of trial and error in running workshops at the Learning Technologies Center and the library, we developed an exciting new model for our workshops that enabled kids who came in for just a few minutes to get a brief introduction to Scratch, while giving those who wanted to stay longer an opportunity to create an interesting project. We call this teaching model *just-in-time.*

Adopting this model shook up and improved the way that the Learning Technologies Center was running workshops in the libraries as well as the way we approached them back in the museum environment. It also improved the individual sessions for the participants, as it prompted instructors to look at the youth they are serving as collaborators in the learning. In the workshop context this means when the instructor doesn't know something or lacks complete information, he or she is encouraged to collaborate with the kids in the session for help. This is a new kind of thinking about teaching, and it gives permission to library staff to run programs even if they don't have all the answers.

This not only helps the librarian-teacher, but it also builds deeper technology skills in youth and models risk taking: the adult in charge exposes that she is not the expert and is comfortable asking for help. The approach has had several other benefits. It has helped us to discover young people who want to contribute what they know, to take on the role of teacher, and it has made the workshop setting much more comfortable by infusing it with a willingness to contribute and a strong community spirit.

CHOOSING THE WORKSHOP FORMAT

Every workshop you offer provides an opportunity for youth to develop and build on a set of critical 21st century skills in the context of positive youth development. With a few caveats, you can plan either formal workshops or open studios that teach Scratch for any age. You will most likely get a mixture of ages (chronological) and stages (experience with technology) in whatever workshop you present. Knowing ahead of time that you'll have a range allows you to plan ahead. Setting realistic expectations for the workshop will give participants, whatever the age or stage, the confidence they need to be successful in learning Scratch and developing projects.

STAND-ALONE OR ONGOING?

Formal workshops and open studios can be developed either as a stand-alone (one shot) experience or as part of an ongoing set of programs. While we use the word stand-alone, we don't mean that the workshop has only one session. A stand-alone formal workshop could be, for example, a three-session game design series that requires all the sessions to complete a specific project. This approach will be most successful when you know you have a group of kids who will sign up and attend all of the sessions. We have found that this doesn't often happen. A youth (or parents) will sign up for all sessions but attend only one or two—and not necessarily in sequence. One way to prepare for this possibility is to make each part of the series stand on its own. In other words, take a scaffold approach to teaching. Whether formal workshops are a single session or a two- to-four-part series that takes place during a short time frame (one to four weeks), they require a set of activities that provide a scaffolded learning experience. They need careful planning so that learning activities are thoughtfully sequenced. Given that programs may need to be marketed up to six months ahead of time, a lot of work must be done before the actual workshop start date.

ONGOING PROGRAMS

Open studios, offered anywhere from once a week to once a month, allow you to develop different and deeper relationships with youth, especially those who are more highly engaged in technology and design. Open studios take a more reflexive approach. You can address more quickly the interests of participants on a week-to-week basis, and while you won't be able to purchase equipment or software as quickly as the kids might like, you can be planning to take advantage of opportunities that arise. We often give our kids the task of finding the appropriate tools and software that address their interests. This shows kids that you are interested in satisfying their needs while also teaching them valuable lessons about making economical choices. It's also good practice for positive youth development.

Ongoing workshops present challenges for marketing and promotion, the largest being what to call such workshops. To be as clear as possible in marketing materials, we call our open studios workshops open tech labs. We describe them as a chance to try out different kinds of software, which we often specify by name. We suggest avoiding any use of the words *game* or *online game* in a description because this creates expectations that can rarely be met with the time and tools available. If you do want to use those terms, be as explicit and sparing in the description as possible. Sometimes using the label *arcade* or *retro* is sufficient. Kids know that these terms hark back to the first video games, like Pong and Pac-Man, which used simpler graphics and much less complex story lines. Understanding this will help kids avoid the expectation that the workshop will teach them how to create modern, highly graphical games with deep narratives, like Halo. Also be careful when planning a program brochure or poster. Too little information or information that is too generic won't be appealing; being too specific takes away the spontaneity and responsiveness of the programs.

TIMING AND SEQUENCING

Once you've determined the type of workshop you'll offer, you need to think about timing and pacing. What's the best way to allow for exploration while taking advantage of teachable moments using the just-in-time method?

FORMAL WORKSHOPS

In planning your formal workshops you will want to set a rhythm that allows for plenty of exploration and discovery. If the workshop is part of a multisession workshop, you will also need to consider the flow between individual sessions and design each with some flexibility. You may be able to move to session two at the tail end of session one, or you may need to extend session one into the second one. But you can start by deciding how many things you actually want to teach during the workshop and deciding how much time you need to allot for each.

We recommend a one-hour workshop minimum (for open studios as well) but encourage you to try for two-hour or even three-hour sessions whenever possible. This doesn't mean you have to be teaching for two to three hours. It only means that you have a fixed set of objectives and allow for plenty of time for kids to experiment and revise. As we mentioned early on, we consider the process of learning as important as the product of the learning. Kids will learn what they need (and want) to learn regardless of what we want them to walk away with.

For a one-hour formal workshop, one or two learning chunks per workshop is probably plenty, particularly if you are working with younger or inexperienced youth. A good first choice may be a simple animation project, like digital greeting cards. Such a workshop can appeal to a wide range of youth or even to families. During the session, participants will learn the basics of working with sprites (the characters in Scratch projects), creating movement (how to create and edit a sprite and how to make it move across the screen), and creating a background. As with any Scratch workshop, the projects that result may be simple or complex. Your goal as the instructor is to provide the necessary tools and support (technical as well as educational) and to avoid getting in the way of a child's learning

We've talked a bit about your stepping back to allow the child to uncover his or her personal learning goals. Your role is more like a mentor than a teacher—engaging in conversations with children as their questions arise, rather than providing all the answers. Knowing how to ask good questions is a lifelong skill that will serve youth well as they grow and learn, and you can model the behavior in your role as teacher-mentor. And as librarians, we know only too well that *how* a question is asked often determines the relevance of the answer. In a sense, our reference interview skills are every bit as important in this type of workshop as elsewhere in our jobs. And implicit in this is having a deep knowledge of how to make it apparent to learners that they can find information in the source at hand, in this case, Scratch.

OPEN STUDIOS

An open studio, which has no specific project goal, works best as a two-hour experience. That doesn't mean you shouldn't have a schedule in mind. First you should spend about ten minutes describing your focus for the day. This could be as simple as talking about the software and tools available or providing complex suggestions about projects that kids might develop. You should also spend five to ten minutes giving a standard introduction to Scratch and how to open and run a project. This provides everyone with a basic foundation from which to work.

Follow up by having the participants introduce themselves and identify what they are interested in exploring. Some children will find this difficult, but it helps build bridges between strangers and helps you see where you will be needed during the workshop. The next hour + is the heart of the workshop. During this time you'll want to keep an eye on what the kids are doing and help them set realistic expectations for themselves and the software tool they are using.

A rough estimate of teaching time for each learning chunk is about twenty minutes, so for a one-hour workshop that teaches two distinct things you'll want to set aside forty minutes. You may want to split the first 20 minutes into two sections and spend ten minutes introducing some basic ideas about programming with Scratch. In the next ten minutes let the kids explore and discover on their own. Then reserve another twenty minutes later on to focus on specific ideas and skills. You'll know that it is time to introduce the next element when kids start to ask questions or get restless. Learners who have been engaged right from the beginning will move ahead at their own pace. You can move on as needed and introduce new elements individually to kids who are ready to proceed before the other participants. Volunteers or other co-teachers can help to manage this effort.

Because we believe sharing and reflection are important, we aim to allow ten to fifteen minutes at the end of a session for kids who are so inclined to show what they have created. We don't push; some kids are shy about their projects and can be uncomfortable if they have not had many experiences talking in public. Regardless of the public display, be sure that you have enough time to visit with each child and comment on his or her project. This recognition is very meaningful, and your conversations will help the children reflect on what they have learned, thus deepening the experience.

Ask questions like, "What do you like best about your project?" or "What was your favorite thing to work on?" Be specific. Rather than saying, "Nice project," give a constructive comment the child can learn from and build on. You might say something like, "I like how you used colors to show how the sprite moves" or "I can see you really spent a lot of time figuring out how to make the timing of the lyrics match the timing of the song." With a little practice, you'll find a positive comment for just about any project. We have found this process essential to building a practice of a supportive learning community.

LONGER FORMAL WORKSHOPS

Timing for longer (over one hour) formal workshops can follow along the same lines, twenty minutes per learning chunk, but you will want to be practical and build in appropriate breaks. In a longer workshop it will be more important to check in regularly with each kid to ensure that he or she remains interested and is keeping up. If most kids are whizzing through the chunks, you can speed things up for everyone; if some are lagging, ask the ones farther along to help with questions.

Because balancing the needs of fast versus slow learners comes up in just about any class or workshop setting, volunteers or additional instructors can be valuable. Within the first ten minutes of class you will be able to assess which kids may need (or request) more direct help and which are explorers. But if you keep in mind that your job is to provide a common approach and a supporting learning environment, you'll see that each kid will get something out of the workshop, even if it isn't the same thing as her neighbor.

Once you've been teaching Scratch workshops for a while, you may want to have the kids self-select into experienced and new users. That makes it easier to help them as you move around the learning space. You can also assign a volunteer to one group and concentrate on the other yourself. At different points in the session you will want to call everyone's attention to the projection screen to explain a particular technique or to demonstrate a new feature. These teachable moments often arise from questions the participants ask, and calling these out is a good way to build competency within the group.

AN EXAMPLE
Sequencing a Game Design Multisession Workshop

SESSION 1

The first session can focus on introducing the concept of games and gaming. You can download a variety of game projects from Scratch that have different features. Kids can spend their time exploring and remixing these games—making simple changes in colors, characters, speed, and the like. In doing so they'll be figuring out how Scratch works and developing ideas for their own projects. Some kids will simply be content to explore. Those who remix can save their modifications to the Scratch website or to a flash drive to retrieve during the next session. You'll probably even have kids who quickly begin their own games. If kids don't come back for the second session, they will have learned some of Scratch's programming basics and how to explore the Scratch website on their own. They can return to Scratch at a later time, in a different setting, or in another session you offer, and have beginner's knowledge on which to build.

SESSION 2

The second session can start by having the kids open the Scratch software and create a simple game—a chasing game, for example. Kids who missed the opportunity to explore games in the first session won't really be at a disadvantage; they will quickly focus on the skill building you will be introducing. Kids who attended the first session will get an in-depth knowledge of Scratch programming. They will have tasted the possibilities through their previous exploration and will be ready either to work again on the project they worked on previously or to begin a new project you are introducing. You'll probably find some kids moving forward much more quickly, ready to incorporate features like scoring and variables. Again, children can save their projects to work on in the next session or consider this session to be a complete experience.

SESSION 3

A third session can provide an opportunity to incorporate even more elements into their project and build greater skills in programming, narrative, graphics, and other facets of game development. As the teacher, you'll be able to help kids new to the group get started using content from sessions one and two, while returning kids work in a more self-directed way. A bonus is that the kids with some experience can mentor those who are new. This is a great example of creating a spiraled learning experience between sessions rather than within one.

HARDWARE AND SOFTWARE

SELECTING COMPUTERS

Scratch workshops can use laptop or desktop computers or even a mixture. If you have the opportunity to purchase computers, or otherwise select between laptop and desktop computers, we strongly encourage the use of laptops. Not only do laptops make it much easier to design your learning space to suit your needs, but their small size allows you to quickly see how well participants are engaged in the workshop. It is easy for people, adults included, to hide behind a desktop, particularly if the monitor is on top of the box. Desktop computers, though, may be more readily available in your facility, particularly if your library has an existing computer lab and will let you get the job done. Future versions of Scratch and other design software may become available for handhelds or tablet computers, but these are not currently available.

One benefit of laptops is that, for the most part, they have built-in microphones, which can be very helpful for expanding the range of content you can teach in a workshop. Another advantage is that laptops are not generally linked to an organization's secure network, so it is easier to get software loaded. Macintosh Windows or even the Linux computers can be used. Scratch was designed for low-end computers, so budget laptops or older desktops were perfectly fine for our programs.

A technology program that focuses on teaching technology skills depends, of course, on the availability of enough of the technology. For eight- to eleven-year-olds, for example, we use a one-to one or one-to-two pairing with the computers. We've found that kids this age tend to be solo learners, so in planning a workshop for them it may be wise to limit the number of kids sharing a computer. This doesn't mean there has to be a one-to-one correspondence between participants and equipment for all workshops. Sharing can be good in more ways than one. Funds for equipment are often scarce, so the less spent on equipment, the better. It also feeds in to the desired outcomes. If creating opportunities for collaboration is one, then having a two-to-one or even a three-to-one ratio of participants to equipment is ideal. The key is to be mindful of your mix of audience and outcomes.

For demonstrating Scratch techniques, showing sample projects, and teaching, you will want a projector. This should be connected to the instructor's computer. A blank wall is sufficient to project onto, but be sure you know if your projector is short or long throw so it can be placed in the best proximity to the screen. Experiment with this before the workshop, sitting in all positions in the workshop room to find out if everyone will be able to see the images on the screen or wall.

Although it is entirely possible to teach without one, a projector gives you a focal point for the room and a way to call participants' attention to key learning moments. You can teach specific skills more easily than you could if you tried to gather participants around one small computer screen. A projector also allows you to invite the kids up to show their projects on a large scale to everyone, which is fun and important for building a sharing community. To facilitate this show and tell, move the projects to flash drives, just in case the Internet connection fails.

ADDITIONAL HARDWARE TOOLS

Many kids, especially those under twelve, enjoy drawing. Scratch makes it easy to incorporate hand-drawn pictures into projects. If you have pencils (graphite and colored), crayons, markers, and high-quality paper on hand kids who love to draw can use them to build a Scratch project. Scanners can then be used to incorporate the hand-drawn pictures into projects. If you're conducting an animation workshop, make a connection to the physical world by having kids make simple flip books out of paper so that they can touch and see what they will be doing with Scratch. This will also help them understand that animation can be explored in many different media.

Use PICO sensor boards or Lego WeDos to create some fun workshops for the tinkerers. These tools make connections with robotics and demonstrate how computers and sensors can interact with the environment by allowing users to create kinetic interactive sculptures or programmable puppets.

Other types of equipment can add greatly to a workshop but will increase the costs of your programs. These include the direct costs for the equipment as well as the additional staff time to learn how to use and incorporate the new tool. Once you've become comfortable with Scratch, you can consider incorporating additional types of technology. This may be part of the original goals you set for your technology programming in your library. Expanding the range of technology you use can grow the types of workshops you offer for each age group and experience level. Your library may be the only place where some kids have a chance to explore with these types of hardware gadgets.

- *Drawing tablets*: Many children, especially eight- to eleven-year-olds, love to draw. Drawing tablets can be a terrific tool that helps these budding artists bring what they are already skillful in to the Scratch environment.
- *Microphones*: Music is tremendously important to many teenagers. Having microphones for teens to record themselves or their friends meets the social needs of this age group. Macintosh computers are another excellent tool for adding music composition and editing to workshops.
- *Digital cameras*: These provide a way for youth to generate their own media for Scratch programs. We've had wonderful success with teaching animation by having kids take pictures of themselves in several sequential positions and

then incorporating these into animation projects. A bonus of digital cameras is that many people are already familiar with using them, so they are easier to introduce than other tools such as drawing boards.

If you are using any of these extras, try to have at least one or two of each item for a group of ten to twelve kids. Having more available runs the risk of skewing the program toward that tool, away from Scratch. For example, giving each kid a camera might turn the program into a digital photography class. While this isn't a bad thing, it does make different demands on the instructor's skill and preparation. This may again be an opportunity to consider the full scope of your technology programming. You may want to hold some workshops to explore each of these additional tools with kids. To support these extras you will want to make sure that you have essentials like extra batteries, spare cables, and memory cards for the cameras.

SOFTWARE

For initial Scratch-based programs the only required software is Scratch. You'll want to make sure the current version of Scratch is available on all computers before the workshop starts. If you haven't been successful in getting it loaded onto your library's image, you'll need to have a supply of flash drives preloaded with Scratch. The files take up about fifty-five megabytes. Flash drives with Scratch installed also allow you to take the workshops to partnering organizations that have computers available but aren't able to have Scratch loaded.

Internet access is highly desirable to allow kids to join the Scratch community, share projects online, and get help with projects, but it is not a requirement to run a successful workshop. Saved projects can be uploaded later to the Scratch site, so immediate Internet access isn't required.

ADDITIONAL SOFTWARE

Although Scratch can stand on its own as a software platform for workshops, you may want to consider incorporating other software into your workshops. These tools allow participants to incorporate other techniques into Scratch projects and help them make connections to the physical world that are so important for deepening learning

Following are additional pieces of open source software and freeware to supplement Scratch workshops. All of these programs are freely available and are tested, stable applications that work well in workshop settings.

- *Audacity* (http://audacity.sourceforge.net/) is a powerful sound editor that can be used to create, record, and edit sounds and music for Scratch projects.

- *Picasa* (http://picasa.google.com), photo-editing software from Google, lets you manipulate images from digital cameras and downloaded from the Web that you can later import into Scratch projects as sprites or backgrounds.
- *ArtRage 2 Starter Edition* (www.artrage.com/artrage-demos.html) is a natural media drawing program. It helps budding and established artists create digital drawings using tools that replicate real media—oil, watercolors, etc.
- *Gimp* (www.gimp.org) is a more advanced image editor. It was designed as a powerful free alternative to the commercial program Photoshop. Gimp lets you create as well as edit images that can be incorporated into Scratch projects.

If you have Macintosh computers, you can also use iPhoto for image editing and Garage-Band for sound and music creation. There are several other freely available software programs you can use to expand your workshops. SAM Animation is a wonderful program that allows users to create stop-motion and time-lapse videos. It is free to use by educational organizations. In addition, there are several software applications for creating narrative projects in 3-D environments. Alice and its sister, Storytelling Alice, are programs from Carnegie Mellon that teach computer programming in 3-D worlds. Starlogo TNG, developed at MIT, makes it easy to create interactive models and simulations in 3-D environments with a building-block programming language similar to Scratch and also based on the Logo language.

These applications are not professional tools, but they are all free, cross-platform (Windows and Macintosh), and well supported. They are also relatively easy to use. Keep in mind that as you incorporate additional software, you increase the level of skill and knowledge required by the instructor. You may need to find additional instructors with knowledge of the new applications. There is a delicate balance between the level of technical skill needed to teach a Scratch-only class and one that incorporates other software. Ultimately, success depends partly on the tools selected, partly on the audience, and partly on the staff you have at hand.

GETTING STARTED USING SCRATCH

What follows in the next chapter is an introduction to the essentials of Scratch. We'd like to stress that although we are providing step-by-step instructions for many projects in the next chapter, you'll want to develop your own approach to teaching what you learn. Discovery and exploration are part of the Scratch experience. If you simply give participants the information we include, you would be discouraging creative exploration and self-directed learning. Think of the next chapter as your reference guide for teaching.

Once you understand the basics, the projects and the templates we present will give you lots of ideas for developing a variety of workshops. Do more than simply read through a project. Practice as you might for a story time; work with timing, pacing, etc. As you go through a project, look for potential problem areas for kids and places where you might want to veer from the established plan. The more workshops you do, the easier it will be for you to spot the potential for kids to get sidetracked or to need extra help.

NOTES

1. Mitchel Resnick, "All I Really Need to Know (About Creative Thinking) I Learned (by Studying How Children Learn) in Kindergarten," in *Proceedings of the Creativity and Cognition Conference*, Washington, DC, June 2007.

2. Ibid.

3. Mitchel Resnick et al., "Scratch Programming for All," *Communications of the ACM* 52, no. 11 (November 2009): 60–67.

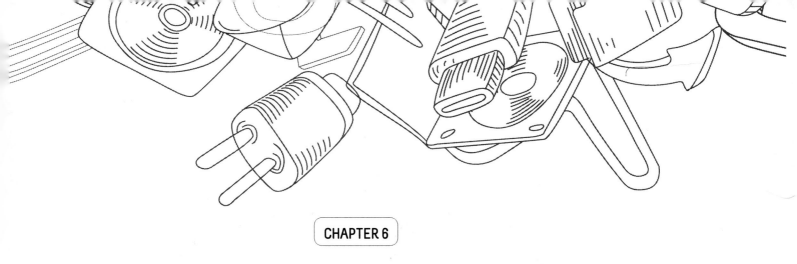

CHAPTER 6

All about Scratch Workshops

I n this chapter we'll outline several types of Scratch workshops that you may want to offer. The projects we introduce are ones that we've had success with in libraries, schools, and at the Science Museum of Minnesota. The instructions, templates, and descriptions are designed to give you the flavor of the project and, we hope, entice you to try them out yourself. But first we will introduce you to the software's structure, basic commands, and key terminology. Then we'll describe the Scratch website and outline how it can be used as a teaching tool and as a venue for youth to showcase their work and participate in a safe online community. The remainder of the chapter will focus on workshop topics and templates. These build on one another, so if you already have some experience with Scratch, you may want to jump ahead to the more complex projects you'll find referenced later in the chapter.

All of the projects in this section can be found in our Scratch Workshop Templates gallery (http://scratch.mit.edu/galleries/view/71644/title/asc), and more information can be found at Media MashUp's ning site (http://mediamashup.ning.com). You may want to download the projects to your computer so you can explore the programming blocks that underlie each while you read through the project descriptions.

MEET SCRATCH: BASIC COMMANDS AND TERMINOLOGY

We have provided you with some basic information about the interface and Scratch terminology, but you'll learn more about Scratch by opening and tinkering with the projects

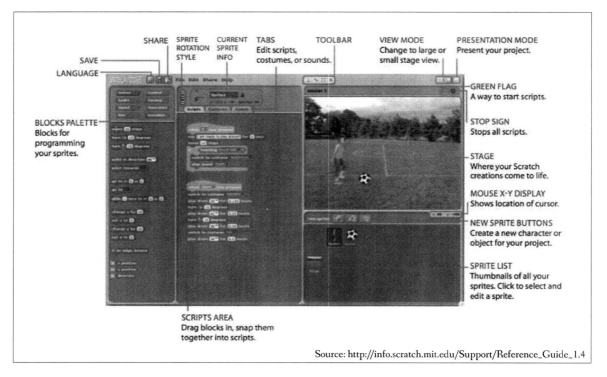

Source: http://info.scratch.mit.edu/Support/Reference_Guide_1.4

FIGURE 6.1   Scratch 1.4 Interface

and by taking a look at the excellent Scratch reference guide. (http://info.scratch.mit.edu/ Support/Reference_Guide_1.4). The guide includes an interface page that highlights the components of the program. (See figure 6.1.)

Our projects are executed in Scratch version 1.4, but because MIT programmers are building subsequent versions of Scratch as backwards compatible, you'll be able to use our lessons even with an earlier (or a future) version. Depending on how you learn best, you might want a print copy to mark up or have the guide up in a second tab in your Internet browser as you work your way through these projects.

Scratch uses a specially developed vocabulary. Table 6.1 defines key terms used in the program. The language used to talk about Scratch projects is also unique. The software was designed to be intuitive for kids, so it uses shapes and colors as key ways to enhance their understanding of how the software works.

We strongly encourage you to use the Scratch website (http://scratch.mit.edu) as a partner in developing your workshops. It is a great place to find ideas. The website's home page, shown in figure 6.2, invites you to create an account and download Scratch free of charge. You can create and share your own ideas on the site and download interesting projects to build a gallery of favorites. By downloading and remixing projects others have posted, you can extend your skills. In addition, the whole process provides a great opportunity to discuss issues related to copyright and intellectual property in a way that really resonates

Table 6.1

KEY TERMS IN SCRATCH

SCRATCH FEATURE	WHAT IT IS
sprite	A sprite is the noun in a project. It is a character that is programmed for activity. It can be an animal, an object, a person, whatever you want.
costume	A costume is like a skin; sprites can be programmed to have many different costumes, which can be changed in infinite ways and an unlimited number of times.
stage	The stage is the background in which the costumed sprite lives. Backgrounds can be programmed with scripts, and different backgrounds can be used in a project.
blocks (programming blocks)	Blocks are the actual program commands.
scripts	Scripts are built from programming blocks and provide instructions to sprites and backgrounds.
scratchr	Scratchr is a Scratch website with forums, help, and hundreds of thousands of projects.
remix	Remix is a technique; any project created in Scratch and loaded to the website can be downloaded by anyone. When a project is modified (remixed) and uploaded back to the site, its code is embedded with a tag that automatically gives credit to the original project creator.

with youth. The Scratch online community is a well-moderated and safe place where your program participants can connect with like-minded individuals across the world and build essential communication skills.

To create a project you will build a set of scripts in Scratch. Each project has scripts related to sprites, the background, and interaction between them. Some are very simple and others quite complex. One of the wonderful things about Scratch is that there is no single right way to create a project. The projects that follow will give you an understanding of the big ideas that form the basis of a workshop.

ANIMATION

Animation projects involve creating or importing sound and images as well as using many kinds of programming blocks. Because animation projects can explore a wide variety of

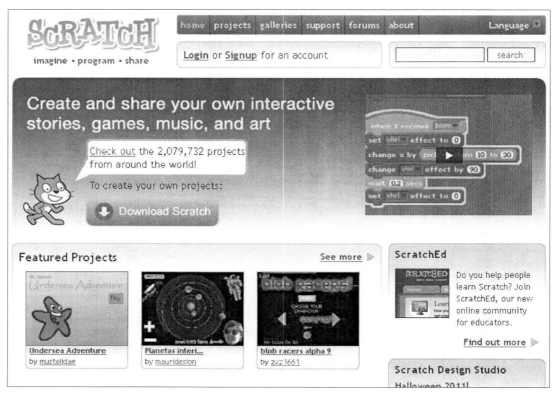

FIGURE 6.2   Scratch Website Home Page

themes, they will work with any age group. The following projects give you a chance to experiment with animation. The basic programming techniques are easy to learn and can pave the way to exploring drawing or music or going deeper into programming.

We use two teaching approaches for our projects; both work well. In the first approach, kids start from scratch (no pun intended). That is, everyone begins with a blank project and builds together. This works best with the simpler projects, which require just a few scripts. The workshop can focus on creating sprites or messages. In the second approach, called remixing, participants download and make changes to an existing project, personalizing it. This approach is often effective for younger children who may feel intimidated by a blank slate. Our role is to help each individual tinker with and personalize aspects of the project by changing the color or the sound, for example.

Remixing is an excellent way to teach more complicated, high-interest projects such as games. This technique allows kids to work at their own speed. The example project files included with the Scratch software download make this easy. You can also download projects from the example gallery (http://scratch.mit.edu/galleries/view/71644/title/asc) to a flash drive, and then upload them to each computer as part of the workshop. Try the following projects yourself, with Scratch open on your computer; then use them with kids.

BEGINNING ANIMATION

A great way to introduce Scratch is by building a simple animation project. The programming techniques are not complicated, and the results are usually fun. Such projects are particularly good for children ages eight to eleven because they balance a few programming commands with drawing. More motivated or skilled participants can easily scale up their projects by adding costumes and scripts or new sprites. We will start this section with instructions for a simple one-hour animation workshop, following up with animation workshops for kids of different ages and interests.

Bring the physical world effectively into the workshop with a flip book. Create ahead of time a couple of very simple ones that the kids can play with. You might enlist the help of a teen advisory group or volunteers (teen or adult). Then ask participants to make their own. Experimenting with flip books will help children (especially those who are concrete learners) better understand animation techniques. Plan on spending fifteen to twenty minutes creating the flip books. Your library may own books on animation that you can bring in to use for reference during the workshop.

The most basic animation is created from two images of the same scene with slightly different positions in each image. In Scratch, children create a sprite with a costume and then copy this costume, making a slight (or dramatic) change to the second costume. This is a great learning moment. You can use it to discuss animation, anime, or cartoons and to explain how artists can create the illusion of movement by rapidly showing images in sequence.

Open Scratch (or click the New button if it's already open). When you first open Scratch, you'll see the screen shown in figure 6.3.

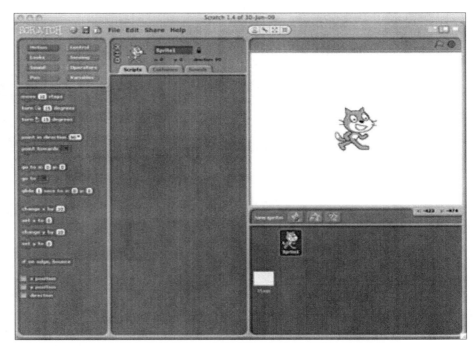

FIGURE 6.3   Scratch Program New Project Screen

Whenever you create a new project in Scratch, you'll start with a cat sprite, but we want participants to make their own drawings. Use the scissors shown on the toolbar in figure 6.4 to cut out the cat, and make a new sprite by clicking on the paintbrush button shown in figure 6.5.

FIGURE 6.5   Paintbrush Button to Create a New Sprite

FIGURE 6.4   Toolbar to Delete Cat Sprite

When the Paint window comes up, click on the smallest magnifying glass to zoom out all the way.(See figure 6.6.) Then play with the different tools shown in figure 6.7: paintbrush, eraser, paint bucket, rectangle tool, ellipse tool, line tool, text tool, select tool, stamp tool, and eyedropper.

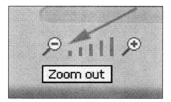

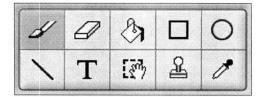

FIGURE 6.6   Zoom Options   FIGURE 6.7   Paint Editor Toolbar

By clicking on Brush Size, shown in figure 6.8, you can change the size of your paintbrush or eraser.

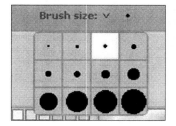

FIGURE 6.8   Brush Size Options

Try drawing a simple object such as a face or bug. Figure 6.9 shows a simple rectangular face.

FIGURE 6.9   Simple Rectangular Face

Even though it's tempting, don't draw in background. Click the OK button when you're satisfied with your simple drawing.

Next we'll look at your sprite's costumes and create another costume to animate your sprite. Click the Costumes tab for your sprite in the center area of the screen, shown in figure 6.10.

FIGURE 6.10   Costumes Tab

This will show the costume you just created. Now click the Copy button (figure 6.11) to make an exact replica.

FIGURE 6.11   Copy Costumes Button   FIGURE 6.12   Edit Costumes Button for Costume 2

Click the Edit button (figure 6.12) to make some small changes to the copy of the sprite (costume2 in this example). Change the shape of the mouth, for example, or add eyebrows. When you click OK you'll see the two costumes of your sprite in the Costumes tab, as shown in figure 6.13.

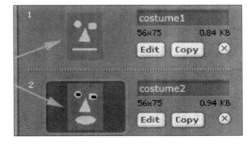

FIGURE 6.13   Showing Edited Costume 2

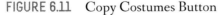

To preview the animation—to see the sprite switch from one face to the other—click once on each costume icon in sequence. Move and click back and forth between the two, and your sprite will animate!

To create a script to animate the sprite on command, click on the Scripts tab (figure 6.14) and drag out blocks to create the program.

FIGURE 6.14   Scripts Tab

Look at the Blocks Palette on the top and click the Looks button shown in figure 6.15. Locate the Switch to Costume <costumename#> block shown in figure 6.16. Click and drag it to the scripts area in the center of the screen.

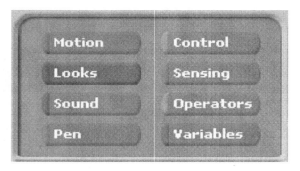

FIGURE 6.15   Blocks Palette

Click on the drop-down arrow next to the name. You'll see a list of all the costumes you created for your sprite.

FIGURE 6.16   Switch to Costumes Block

Go back to the Blocks Palette and select Control. Scroll until you find the Wait block. Click and drag this to the Scripts area and snap it under Switch to Costume. Repeat to make the group of blocks shown in figure 6.17.

One of the blocks is named costume1; the other is costume2 (the names in your project may be different). Next change the wait time from 1 second to 0.1 seconds by clicking in the Scripts box and typing in 0.1.

FIGURE 6.17   Script of Costume Blocks

Pull out a Forever block from Control. Then drag the whole script inside the Forever block as shown in figure 6.18. A little white line ("glue") shows up when the script is close enough to stay put.

FIGURE 6.18   Forever Block around Costume Blocks

Okay! From the Control blocks, drag out the Green Flag block and snap it on top of the Forever block. Placing it here will cause your animation to start when you click the Green Flag button shown in figure 6.19.

FIGURE 6.19   Green Flag "Run" Block

FIGURE 6.20   Green Flag Button

Click the Green Flag button and your animation sequence will move on its own until you click the Stop button. (See figure 6.20.)

Congratulations! You've created a Scratch animation.

BLUE KITTY WORKSHOP

Now that you know the basics of animation, try it out with Blue Kitty, a one-hour workshop (http://scratch.mit.edu/projects/keithbraafladt/872776). This project starts with a simple hand-drawn blue cat sprite that has four costumes; each costume shows the cat's tail in a different position. Using four costumes lets the animation happen much more smoothly. We like this particular workshop because it focuses only on changes in one part of the costume—the tail—which makes it a good project for eight- to eleven-year-olds. You might want to start with a hands-on activity such as having kids create tails out of paper or yarn and observe the motions as they are swinging them.

Here's how you can structure the timing within the workshop to make sure you are able to introduce all the project's parts. The underlying idea is to introduce the idea, or learning element, you want them to learn, and give the kids a chance to experiment with it; then introduce the next learning element, and so on. Some kids will work faster than others, but as you are moving through the room helping out, you'll figure this out and find the kids who need more attention.

Spend the first ten minutes sharing and talking about paper flip books you bring in or experimenting with paper models they created. Have the kids draw their initial cat for the next fifteen or twenty minutes. Some kids will focus on the details of their drawing, while others will jump into playing with motion and costume blocks that make the costumes move. Spend another ten minutes editing and creating the second costume, and then another fifteen minutes showing the motion blocks and programming the costume switch. Invite the kids to share their creations in the last ten minutes.

ADVANCED ANIMATION

DAYDREAM WORKSHOP

DayDream (http://scratch.mit.edu/projects/keithbraafladt/872779) is a great example of an advanced animation project. The project works very well with both tweens and teens. It incorporates hand-drawn images that were scanned and imported into Scratch. The drawings are simple sketches, and the backgrounds are hand-drawn. Music is also played in the background. This project demonstrates that drawings created in the real world can quickly be transferred to Scratch and brought to life through scripts and music, which can set a different tone for a drawing. The idea is to create an environment that lets kids use their ability to draw that they already have to help them acquire new skills in computer design and programming. Allow two hours for the experience.

Since older youth are often already comfortable with hand-drawing, this workshop gives you the opportunity to slow the pace and bring in additional technology. Because the program centers on drawings done by hand, you will need to ensure that the participants can draw comfortably. We don't usually draw with something the size of a computer mouse; normally we use a pencil, so, if possible, you'll want to provide a better drawing implement. The touch pad on a laptop is actually a great alternative to a mouse; drawings can be done with one finger. Graphics tablets are wonderful if you have some available. If you want participants to be able to use traditional media—such as paper and pencils—you'll need a scanner and a digital camera to digitize their drawings. You'll need to use Artrage (www .artrage.com/artrage-demos.html) or something similar with this project, so you will want to give kids a few minutes to become familiar with the tool. If you have a volunteer available for this session, have him or her help participants with Artrage or the scanner while you explain the full project.

For this session plan on forty to sixty minutes for drawing and scanning, uploading and editing, and, finally, importing images into Scratch. If you decide on the draw-and-digitize approach, balance the activities to account for additional time to use a scanner and image-editing software. The hand-drawn and imported art may need to be resized or cleaned up to look good in a Scratch project. You can use free programs such as Picasa or Gimp to do this. The remainder of the session (sixty to eighty minutes) can be spent animating the drawings and adding a soundtrack and timing.

FIGURE 6.21   New Sprite Button

Be sure you explore all the programs beforehand and know enough about them to show kids how to prepare their images for Scratch; or recruit a volunteer to help with this. Once a hand-drawn image (or a digital photo) file is on the computer, it can be imported into Scratch. Save image files to the computer desktop to make it easy for everyone to be able to locate and import them.

Create a new sprite by clicking on the new sprite button shown in figure 6.21.

You'll get the Paint Editor toolbox; click the Import button shown in figure 6.22.

FIGURE 6.22   Import Button

The next window prompts you browse to find the file on your computer. Remember to save media to the desktop and it will be easy to import into Scratch—just click the Desktop button shown in figure 6.23.

Scratch will display thumbnails so you can preview the image if you have several to search through. Find your file and click OK. This should open your selected image in the Paint Editor toolbox. You can edit your image (which is now a sprite) to get it ready to use. (See figure 6.24.)

FIGURE 6.23   Desktop Button

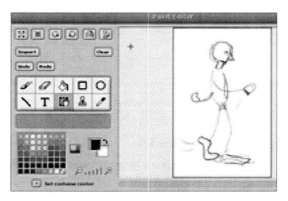

FIGURE 6.24   Image for Editing into Sprite

When you've finished editing your image, click OK and you have your sprite (drawing) on the stage, as shown in figure 6.25. If you create several drawings of your character in different positions for this sprite, you can import these just as you did in the simple animation project.

FIGURE 6.25   Sprite on Stage

Click the Costumes tab to import more drawings. (See figures 6.26 and 6.27.)

FIGURE 6.26   Costumes Tab

FIGURE 6.27   Import Tab

Having youth start projects using traditional tools and media (paper and markers, for example) and then importing them into Scratch—a process called draw and digitize—gives you much more flexibility and can transform the workshop from a technology-focused experience to an art-based experience. The focus on drawing may encourage more girls to participate in your technology programs.

CAVEMAN SLAPSTICK! WORKSHOP

In response to the young people's interest in creating a more sophisticated game like the online game Runescape, we created Caveman Slapstick! (http://scratch.mit.edu/projects/keithbraafladt/872781), which is probably best suited for teens ages fourteen to eighteen. We've mentioned the amount of work involved in creating a simple animation or game, let alone a game as complicated as Runescape, but kids still want to try to create their own versions of games. It's sometimes difficult to convince them of program limitations. Respecting their interests and goals, however, will help you to build stronger relationships with the kids, as well as promote positive youth development.

Caveman Slapstick! is an animation project that uses multiple drawings in sequence from a particular point of view (an isometric view) to create a 3-D appearance. Drawing characters in 3-D is time consuming because each position needs to be drawn out from several different angles.

Scratch has a very simple set of graphics tools, but as Caveman Slapstick! shows, the program can incorporate graphics designed in more sophisticated drawing programs for higher-level animation and, with scripting in Scratch, produce amazing 3-D character motion. The objective of Caveman Slapstick! is to teach skills needed for more complex animation—for example, making movement smoother by adding additional frames and using point-of-view drawings for 3-D effect. Kids also learn how to import sets of images (3-D character animations) to create even smoother and more advanced animation. We have found one especially good (and free) resource to help children explore the world of 3-D drawing. Reiner's Tilesets (www.reinerstilesets.de/) , a website created by German artist Reiner Prokein, allows access to 3-D drawings of many types of characters in multiple animated positions, which can be downloaded and then imported as sprite costumes in Scratch. Caveman Slapstick! uses ten separate drawings from this site to capture the motion of a caveman falling down.

Figures 6.28 and 6.29 are different frames in a sequence that shows a character falling. They are isometric—from a particular point of view—so they also work well in 2-D programs like Scratch.

There are many different characters to choose from on Reiner's website, each with different poses and movements. Several possibilities are shown in figure 6.30.

FIGURE 6.28   Character Falling   FIGURE 6.29   Character Falling

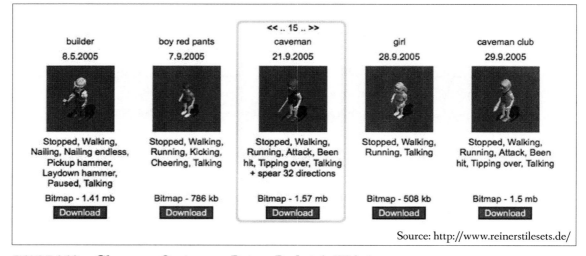

FIGURE 6.30   Character Options on Reiner Prokein's Website

Once you've selected the movement you want and downloaded a set of costume images, just import the individual images as costumes for your sprite, as shown in figure 6.31. This is the same importing process described in DayDream, but with many more images. Several image options are displayed in figure 6.32.

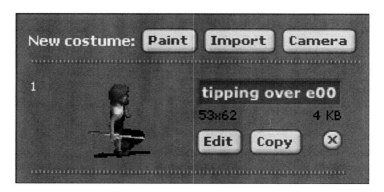

FIGURE 6.31   Importing First of Multiple Images as a Costume

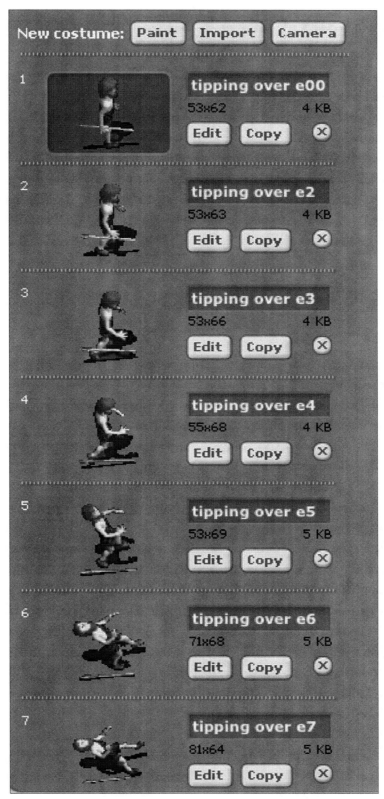

FIGURE 6.32 View of Multiple Images for Animating Sprite

BEYOND ANIMATION

The previous projects demonstrated how to draw and import sprites and build scripts. By now you and your workshop participants have gained familiarity with Scratch's interface and its basic tools and become well versed in the fundamentals of animation. Now we'll describe some additional projects that can form the basis of workshops in your library.

In this section we'll walk through workshops with project templates to give you an idea of what kids will learn and to start you thinking about how you'll develop your own programs. The projects and templates were developed as part of Media MashUp, and we would like to thank Janet Piehl, Hilary Pesson, Cynthia Matthias, and Sabrina Sutliff-Gross for contributing to their creation. Step-by-step templates are located at the end of the chapter.

TELLING PERSONAL STORIES IN SCRATCH

ALL ABOUT ME WORKSHOPS

Scratch is an effective platform for exploring writing of all kinds—reflective, responsive, story extenders, and interactive. Writing with Scratch isn't about developing grammar or sentence structure, so you don't have to be an English teacher to encourage youth to be expressive. What you do need is the ability to encourage them to think deeply about topics that are important to them. Storytelling is about the intersection of images and words. In Scratch, writing is also about coordinating those images and words over time.

Kids of all ages like to talk about themselves and their interests and passions. The All About Me project can be used to create an autobiography. All participants can work with the same elements (What school do you go to? Who is in your family? What is your favorite book, food, or type of music?), or you can encourage them to explore a personal interest more deeply, such as horses, musicians, a favorite place to visit, books, or authors.

All About Me–type workshops are good for ages eight and up. They don't require any extra hardware or software, and they can be run in an hour. Children will create a project that imports spoken words (if microphones are available) and other sounds, or just speech bubbles. They will make (or import) digital images and program the scripts to transition between sprites and backgrounds. The projects can include many different elements or just a few. To begin the workshop you can ask participants to show or describe a favorite object that will be featured in their project. This is a nice way to start building a community of learners. Allow children time to sketch out a storyboard for their narrative on paper. Keke's All About Me (10-keke-allaboutme http://scratch.mit.edu/projects/keithbraafladt/872825) is a good starter example, as is the Charles River Walk project

(12-charlesriverwalk.sb http://scratch.mit.edu/projects/keithbraafladt/872829). This project was made as an alternative to drawing a self-portrait; it's about a place that is meaningful to the creator.

PHOTOFACE WORKSHOP

This project allows participants to use a digital camera, either built-in or external, to create a funny animation. It works well with ages 8 and up. Each person takes a picture of him- or herself and imports it as a background. He then picks a facial feature—eye, nose, mouth— and uses it to create a new sprite. By placing the feature sprite over any part of his face, he can create an image with three eyes, two noses, or two mouths. Some kids will quickly excel at animating the parts of their face and will move on to editing their feature sprites or the background using Scratch's Paint Editor, as Willzuma did in his project (http://scratch .mit.edu/projects/keithbraafladt/1278454). Because some people are self-conscious and reluctant to draw themselves (younger children less so than teenagers or adults), PhotoFace may work best with groups who have an established relationship and high degree of comfort with you and one another. Keke's Making Faces (17-keke-making-faces.sb http://scratch.mit .edu/projects/keithbraafladt/1278449) and Fotoface (18-fotoface.sb http://scratch.mit.edu/ projects/keithbraafladt/1278454) are two additional projects to review.

GAMES AND GAMING

As we mentioned earlier, most young people have misconceptions about what goes into making a computer game. They have limited understanding of the long hours and very large budgets that go into creating games like Halo or Mario Kart. Aiming to create such a project in an informal, drop-in, or even a three-session set of workshops isn't practical. Describing the realities of major game development for youth helps them to better understand why it isn't possible to re-create this type of project in Scratch.

Although free and low-cost game development software (called game engines) is available, we've found Scratch appeals to a wider audience and requires less expertise to teach than game-engine software. As you become more comfortable and proficient using a tool like Scratch (and if demand for more sophisticated project warrants), you may want to introduce more specialized software to meet the interests of kids attending your workshops.

Our advice: By all means offer the classes you can support, but be mindful of the fact that the game-engine software (or professional-quality animation software) doesn't necessarily offer the same literacy skill-building opportunities as a rich media content program such as

Scratch. If you decide to focus on games, you'll also be selling your program to a more limited set of participants, most likely boys. Our Scratch workshops, on the other hand, attract
almost as many girls as boys.

The game projects we provide foster media literacy. Our kids really begin to understand
the variety of components that make up a game and how they interact.

A SIMPLE VIDEO GAME WORKSHOP

Designing a Video Game, a two- to three-hour formal workshop for thirteen- to fifteen-year-
olds, provides a learning opportunity that focuses on iterative problem solving. It allows youth
to experiment and use trial and error to see what happens if . . . Playing video games is the
norm for youth of this age. They play them alone and together, in person and online. We all
know how popular video games are and how connected to status and entertainment they
can be. Kids not only want to be good playing them, but they also want to create games of
their own. Scratch is a great platform for creating a first generation arcade-style game such
as Pong, Asteroids, or even Pac-man.

A successful technique to provide a hands-on connection in this kind of workshop is to
bring in an earlier generation gaming system such as an Atari arcade system. You can also
bring in an inexpensive retro game system, one in which a number of classic video games
have been put into a small video game toy. These are inexpensive, easy to find, and actually
replicate the classic games in an accessible toy for demonstration. Workshop participants
can then play, talk, and share experiences that they might transfer to their computer game
creation.

Building projects from a simple game platform also allows kids to bring their creative ideas
into a safe forum for exploration. We have been careful to focus on the classic, simple game
models because the more recent games are usually far too complex to tackle in an informal
setting. Once kids have designed their games (and had others in the workshop play them),
they can post them to the Scratch community website, where they'll get feedback from
other users. This is a great way for kids to extend the experience and engage in a community
beyond themselves—another developmental asset.

One early set of library workshops we offered focused on video game making. We
introduced each workshop by having teens play with classic arcade games on classic game
consoles: Nintendo and Atari game systems. We recognized that a lot of classic games have
endured through the years, remaining relevant even today. When we took the console systems out and had kids play, we asked how they learned the game so quickly. They answered
that they knew what the games were, and they were familiar with the form. We used this
familiarity as the basis for exploring games in Scratch. Designing a workshop around just

one of these games provides a great opportunity to talk about the specific elements of video games—from narrative, characters, and music to scoring, lives, and levels. Developing an interactive game, however, can be at once fairly complex and very straightforward.

To get around this, we don't spend a lot of time or effort creating complex graphics. Instead, we concentrate first on developing game engines, or the dynamics of game play, which the classic games do so well. After kids become skilled in that area, we can spend additional time on the graphics (character design and backgrounds) and the game's narrative. There are probably thousands of game-focused projects on the Scratch website, so picking one to remix and start with can be difficult and a bit daunting. One of the best starter game projects is based on the familiar Pong Game (05-Ponggame.sb) http://scratch .mit.edu/projects/keithbraafladt/872791). It is effective in teaching the basic principles of interactive games. The player controls one sprite (a paddle), while the other sprite (a ball) is programmed to move randomly on the screen. The project introduces the idea of variables, using the keyboard to control a sprite and to control the outcome. Elements used in other video games, such as timing and scoring, can be incorporated in this game. The Butterfly Game (04-Butterflygame.sb) (http://scratch.mit.edu/projects/keithbraafladt/872790) is another version of a basic game, which appeals to both girls and boys.

We created a simple template to introduce the game dynamics: a player, a goal or something to avoid; a clock of some sort to keep track of time elapsed; a scoring mechanism; and a way to signal when a participant wins or loses. Kids are so familiar with high-quality graphical games that we think it's important to explain again that although participants will get a good start on creating their own games, they won't immediately re-create the type of games they enjoy at home. The template at the end of this chapter makes game creation approachable for children as young as eight or ten.

ADDING SCRIPTS AND BLOCKS

The following projects explore more advanced programming skills. They involve learning additional programming language (blocks) and mathematical concepts. Use remixing to engage younger or inexperienced users quickly, and use the start-from-scratch approach for older or more experienced participants. The templates for both of the following projects are at the close of this chapter.

DRAWING WITH CIRCLES WORKSHOP

Many of us remember the Spirograph drawing kit that let us use pens, paper, and gears to create symmetrical line drawings. Rotating different-size gears made different-size circles and ovals that overlapped in different places. Changing the pen color let us create textured drawings in a controlled yet fluid way.

Drawing with Circles in Scratch is no different. If you can find a toy based on this idea, bring it in. It makes a nice contrast to the screen-based experience and will engage younger kids to do some hands-on work. The project introduces a deeper understanding of movement and the interplay of color. In using Scratch to create drawings kids can explore how to create circles by combining lines and angles or even with squares or triangles.

Once kids become familiar with the basic programming scripts that create circles, they can introduce other elements. They can build scripts that add new colors or change the width of the pen for thicker or thinner lines. Scripts can be created that randomly change the color of the pen or change the color with a special keystroke or command. The examples we list, a mix of simple and more complex projects, will give you a sense of the full range of options for Drawing with Circles workshops.

Plan Drawing with Circles as a two- to three-hour workshop regardless of the age and stage you're planning to invite. You can use our template as a basis for workshops with younger youth, and have them start by downloading and remixing one of our examples, Simple Spiro (19-simplespiro.sb http://scratch.mit.edu/projects/keithbraafladt/1278465), More Spirographing (20-morespirographing.sb http://scratch.mit.edu/projects/keith braafladt/1278471), or Spiral (21-spiral.sb http://scratch.mit.edu/projects/keithbraaf ladt/1278473). If you choose the remix route, spend some time yourself remixing several projects to get a sense of which elements will be easiest for kids to alter. Colors? Speed? The choice is yours, but be sure you know enough to give good direction to kids who might need it.

VARIABLES AND RANDOM NUMBERS

Fortune-telling workshops, which fall neatly into this category, allow kids to learn about and play with variables and random numbers in a variety of ways. Even very simple toys can provide a context for a such a workshop. Janet Piehl, a children's librarian at the Wilmette (IL) Public Library did a fun (two- to three-hour) program for eight- to eleven-year-olds incorporating the Magic 8-Ball toy, the black fortune-telling toy. She brought several Magic 8-Balls to the workshop so the kids could play with them. This hands-on experience helped them understand what the Magic 8-Ball is and how it works before moving on to designing one in Scratch.

Using the physical prop allowed the group to deconstruct what a Magic 8-Ball does and to experiment with question-and-answer scenarios. (If you're unfamiliar, you may want to play with one yourself.) They developed a deeper understanding of the design elements that would need to be part of their Scratch project. They talked about what variables were and how to create a random choice, how the image of the ball would need to move on the screen, and what the ball would need to look like.

The resulting projects were a delightful array of ideas and included variations such as the Monkey Magic 8-Ball project. This workshop was successful in bridging the physical and virtual worlds, teaching Scratch skills, and addressing the developmental stage of the kids to make physical or concrete understandings. It also had the bonus of appealing to girls as well as boys.

Fortune-telling projects are highly interactive, letting kids play with questions and answers much like the paper origami fortune-teller so popular in elementary schools. When you play with the paper fortune-tellers, the questioner picks a number to generate the answer. The fortune-teller opens and closes the folded paper that number of times, and the questioner chooses the flap to open. Bringing in paper and letting the kids experiment with the origami version may makes it easier for them to understand the principles of randomness and variables.

The Scratch-created virtual fortune-teller (06-Fortuneteller.sb http://scratch.mit.edu/projects/keithbraafladt/872798) works in the same way. There are a limited number of answers to an unlimited number of questions, which can be funny, thoughtful, irreverent, or sarcastic. While the answers seem random (they aren't meant to actually answer the question), there is a set path for the way the response is generated. The script in the fortune-telling orb version (07-Magic8ball.sb http://scratch.mit.edu/projects/keithbraafladt/872803) is written with a random number variable. A virtual shake of the ball picks the number that houses the answer.

The fortune-telling projects use more complex blocks and scripts and introduce the idea of broadcasting in addition to variables. For example, in the Magic 8-Ball project the Ask block prompts for questions and the Answer blocks are written to provide them. The Broadcast block is used to send instructions from one sprite to another, making sure that actions happen in the right sequence. Sound is programmed to run while the fortune-teller is thinking up an answer. Kids will have fun trying out various question-and-answer scenarios, or they can create a new look for the fortune-teller or experiment with randomness.

MORE PROJECT IDEAS

There are dozens more projects and workshops you may want to consider; we've just scratched the surface. To help you on your way we've created a gallery on the Scratch website with additional projects. We'll describe them here and you can download any of them from the Getting Started—Program Ideas gallery (http://scratch.mit.edu/galleries/view/67110). You might want to develop a workshop around remixing one of these projects or another one you've downloaded from the Scratch website. All Scratch projects are protected by a Creative Commons ShareAlike license, which means you can comfortably (and legally) download, remix, and upload projects. Scratch projects are embedded with code that gives credit to the original project creator. You can use the scripts as they are or modify them to suit your interests. Decide what you want the kids to focus on. Is it the image or the message? If you're feeling especially adventuresome, create your own original project and have the kids remix it!

DIGITAL GREETING CARD WORKSHOPS

Even though our culture is moving away from the handwritten letter, greeting cards retain their popularity. And, as with so many other things, they have moved to the virtual world. Scratch greeting cards can have all kinds of engaging features. They can incorporate sound, prompt the recipients to answer a funny question, or invite them to enter their name to get a personalized greeting. Whether they are simple or complex, greeting cards can brighten anyone's day.

Begin a workshop by bringing in a variety of cards—ones with sparse text, ones that have a sound chip, joke cards, serious cards—and let the kids decide who they'd like to send a card to and what kind of message to include. You can plan one of these workshops around a holiday like Thanksgiving to tie into seasonal programming. Check out Kristen's GoodBye (http://scratch.mit.edu/projects/keithbraafladt/872824) and Hello Kitty (http://scratch.mit.edu/projects/keithbraafladt/872813) for two different examples.

CONTENT-BASED WORKSHOPS

Content-based workshops usually revolve around a specific subject rather than a programming technique or the use of a particular tool. At the Science Museum of Minnesota, for example, we often create a workshop around an exhibit or a research subject that's of topical interest. For youth-based workshops we choose a subject area and create a context using materials and resources from around the museum. The kids will then build projects that explore the subject. Context-based workshops can be built around an event, a holiday, or even current news. As the Chilean miners were being rescued from months underground in 2010, kids were creating projects that celebrated their return to freedom, for example. Imagine a workshop on banned books in celebration of Banned Books Week, or one focusing on Children's Book Week, or Women's History Month. How about a library scavenger hunt in Scratch?

These workshops involve a mixture of research on the subject and skill building with Scratch, during which participants learn how to mediate or re-present images, drawings, sounds, recordings, and music to explore their area of interest. The projects can be writing-, animation-, or game-based, or something else entirely. Our Getting Started—Program Ideas gallery has two examples of content-based projects.

The first example is called Detective Class (http://scratch.mit.edu/projects/keithbraaf ladt/299926). This is actually a template project that was developed specifically for teachers who already had a basic understanding of Scratch. We used Scratch to create an interactive narrative mystery that needed to be solved. The Detective Class Scratch project was based on a real-life participatory mystery that the museum set up for the students' visit. The students participated in a staged drama in which they solved a mystery—an item was stolen from a room—as a dramatic hands-on introduction to the Scratch workshop. The thinking behind this program was to bring together both a physical-social experience and a mediated (in this case, through Scratch) virtual experience.

Prior to the visit, staff carefully created a physical tableau that the class would visit, observe, and gather evidence from, just like a detective might in a crime scene. In this case, the students explored the scene before and after the "crime" (a stolen item from an office desk), noting the state of the scene before the crime and then returning to explore the evidence and clues left behind by the criminal. The kids then developed hypotheses to explain what had happened and tested their powers of observation. They jotted notes and discussed their ideas as a group. Museum staff had created a Scratch template project that included a skeletal structure for a game that was scripted (programmed) to reveal a before-and-after scene with different sorts of clues and changes as evidence of the crime.

When it was their turn to transition to Scratch, the students used a template and added visual elements to the crime scene that would be revealed or hidden depending on each student's own interest in what the crime would be. In the project template we showed before-and-after scenes of an office desk covered with items that may or may not have been stolen. Uncovering the crime scene through the Scratch project took the form of a game that could be played by others. What is nice about this example is that it mixes a media experience designed for the computer screen (images of the before and after scenes of the office desk) with program scripts that are designed to respond to player interaction.

GREAT LAKES WORKSHOP

In our second content-based workshop (http://scratch.mit.edu/projects/keithbraaf ladt/811621) participants were set to explore the history and geography of the Great Lakes in North America as the basis of their Scratch project. Much like a school report, Scratch let the youth incorporate media and programming to tell a story about a particular place and time in history. What's nice about this approach is that because you're describing actual events, you can include not just narrative, but also representations and simulations. These can be animations or data-driven representations, such as boats moving across bodies of water and particular geographic locations.

STOP-MOTION ANIMATION WORKSHOPS

Stop-motion projects are popular with kids of all ages and depend on the availability of digital photos. These projects bring to life Scratch's wide walls by bringing in digital photos taken by the participant or downloaded from free Internet sites. The principles of stop-motion projects are similar to animation and encourage the development of media literacy and technology literacy.

Our gallery has three examples of stop-motion projects. The first (http://scratch.mit.edu/projects/keithbraafladt/811683) is fairly straightforward. We used digital cameras to create stop-motion animation in a Scratch project. We photographed Cynthia Runs (a librarian at Hennepin County) in a series of movements to capture motion. She posed for photographs in three separate positions to represent stages of a person walking. These were imported into Scratch and programmed to show the images in sequence to replicate walking. What's nice is that this project needed only three imported images to create the illusion of movement. Once the Cynthia sprite gets to the side of the Scratch window, the programming lets her flip 180° and move in the opposite direction. So instead of requiring three additional, different images, the programming scripts simply turn the images the other way.

Stop Motion Cars (http://scratch.mit.edu/projects/keithbraafladt/811698) is our second example. Made up of images of cars that simulate moving around a circuit, this racing project uses backgrounds in an interesting way. The images are imported into Scratch as background sprites. The script animates the background and changes one background to the next, to the next, and so on as the car moves around an imaginary track.

Our final example, called Perched (http://scratch.mit.edu/projects/keithbraafladt/811703), combines sprites and screen drawing with interesting digital images (backgrounds) that are imported from the Internet. This example is quite striking, but it requires a solid understanding of how stop-motion works before you can set up the photographs. Moving objects even small distances within the frame creates the illusion of movement when a viewer looks at the sequence of images.

WHAT'S NEXT? MONDAY AND SOME DAY

We hope these projects have given you some specific ideas about how you can use Scratch to create technology-based programs for the youth who come to your library. By becoming Scratchers the kids you work with develop an important set of skills that will serve them well across their lifetime. Your library will benefit by helping them develop those skills in a safe and welcoming environment.

By the end of the Media MashUp project we'd held hands-on workshops introducing Scratch to close to 250 librarians from across the United States. After every workshop the excitement about using Scratch was palpable. Each time we ran a workshop we had conversations with participants who were eager to take the next step and develop a workshop for the kids they serve. The creativity we heard was inspiring and got us to think about how we could support their interest. So we'd ask, "What are you going to do Monday (tomorrow) to help kids take the next step?" Your Monday answer may be to experiment with the projects we've described, or to visit the Scratch website to investigate the range of projects. Maybe it will be to bring your knowledge back to the youth volunteers you work with and get them to help you figure out the next step. Or maybe it will be to work with your IT department to get the software installed on staff computers. There are no right answers. Our suggestion is to do what will help you become more comfortable with Scratch and decide how technology workshops can help you serve youth in your community.

The second question we always ask is, "What are you going to do some day?" What do you aspire to do in three months, six months, or a year? What will it take for you to get there? Do you need to get other staff on board? Do you need to develop a grant proposal to get additional funding to pursue a larger project with other partners? Again, there are no right answers. You know your organization, and we hope we've given you enough information to help you work within it to establish technology programming for youth that is grounded in 21st century literacy skill development.

Appendix to Chapter 6

Project Templates

ALLABOUTME—ANIMATION

This simple introduction to Scratch for youth (ages 8 – 17) and adult educators quickly provides a personal connection to the software, tools, and media resources. You will draw and animate a simple self-portrait and then add a background using Scratch's image files.

👍 LEARNING GOALS

Develop comfort and fluency in creating and manipulating media, express ideas using language, learn the technique of remixing rich media and, finally, develop a personal connection to Scratch by exploring and experimenting with its features.

GET STARTED

 Open Scratch; a new blank file with a cat **sprite** will be created. We're going to make our own characters, so with your mouse, right-click (or on a Mac control-click) on the cat sprite and click **delete** to remove it.

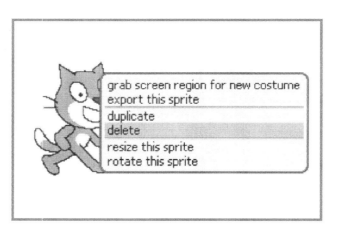

 Make a new sprite by clicking on the **Paintbrush-star** button. This will open the Paint Editor window.

CREATE A SPRITE

  Draw your own sprite: before you begin drawing, zoom out. *Don't paint a background yet.* Experiment with brush size and other tools. Click the **OK** button when you're satisfied with your simple drawing.

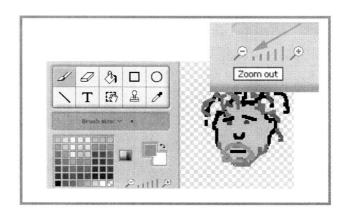

MAKE A COSTUME FOR YOUR SPRITE

 Click the **Costumes** tab for your sprite. This shows the costume you just created. Click the **Copy** button and make an exact copy.

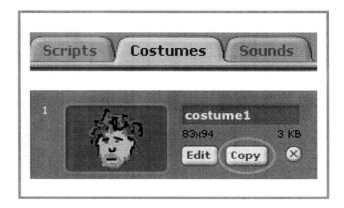

 Next to the copy of the drawing ("costume2" in this case) click the **Edit** button.

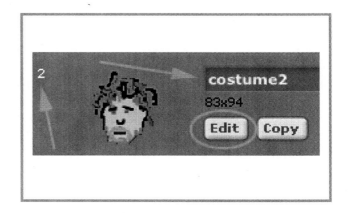

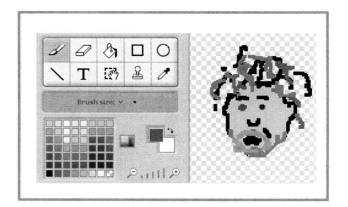 Make some small changes to "costume2"—to the mouth, to the eyes—to show the face moving with speech.

ANIMATE IT

7 Click **OK** and you'll see your sprite's two costumes. To preview the animation, click once on each costume icon, back and forth between the two and your sprite will animate.

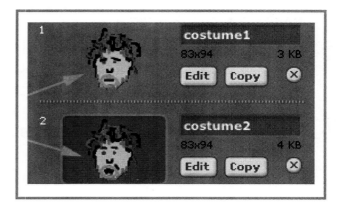

CREATE A SCRIPT

8 Next we want to create a script to make the sprite animate. We'll do this by clicking on the **Scripts** tab and dragging out blocks to create our program. Click the **Looks** button and drag out two *switch to costume#* blocks.

If you click on the little black arrow next to the name, you will see a list of the names of all your costumes. Make one block for "Costume1" and one for "Costume2."

9 From the Control blocks, grab two *wait* blocks. Add these and stack your blocks together, waiting for the white glue line to show up. Change the wait time in each *wait* block by double-clicking on the number and typing 0.1.

ADD A LOOP

10 Drag out a *forever* block and move it onto your script. The *forever* block's "mouth" will open up to surround the blocks then get a *when green flag clicked* block and snap it on top.

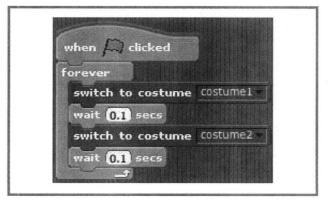

96

SAY SOMETHING ABOUT YOURSELF

11 Now let's say something. Go to Looks, and drag out and snap together three *say Hello! for 2 sec* blocks. You can click on the word "Hello" to highlight and add your message.

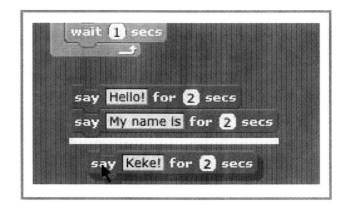

12 Put a *forever* block around the say script and cap with another *when green flag clicked* block.

ADD A BACKGROUND

13 Finally, you'll want to create a setting for your animated self-portrait. To do this, you'll need to create or import an image for the background. To switch to the Stage, click on the Stage icon in the sprites area.

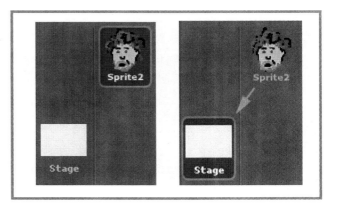

14 Then, in the center scripts area, click on the **Backgrounds** tab, We're going to import an image.

Scratch comes with a great selection of images to use that are copyright free.

This will bring you into the backgrounds folder in Scratch. From here you can choose an image to use for your project.

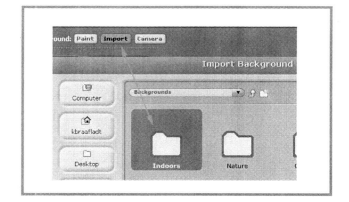

Explore the available backgrounds. Once you find one that you like, click OK to choose it. Now you have the setting for your project!

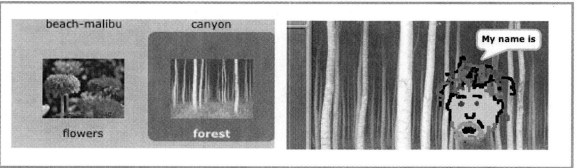

This project begins to explore narrative in Scratch, storytelling, and multiple frame animation seen in projects like the DayDream project in the examples folder – **02-DayDream** (http://scratch.mit.edu/projects/keith-braafladt/872779)

CHECK IT OUT!

This document is supported in part by a grant from the Institute of Museum and Library Services. Any views, findings, conclusions or recommendations expressed in this document do not necessarily represent those of the Institute of Museum and Library Services.

Charlotte Mecklenburg Library • Free Library of Philadelphia • Memphis Public Library • Seattle Public Library • Wilmette Public Library

SCRATCH PHOTOFACE

In this project you'll be able to bring new tools into Scratch by importing a photo of yourself, then animate it using the graphic effects blocks in the Looks section of the Scratch programming blocks.

 LEARNING GOALS

Photoface works great with a range of ages of youth, who are often more comfortable than adults in altering and sharing digital images of themselves. One of the ideas that is integrated into the Scratch application is that it's made to be a tool for expression. Scratch helps the learner to transform their personal experiences through media, using computer programming.

GET STARTED

 Using a built-in webcam or digital camera, take a picture of yourself and save it on the desktop of your computer.

 Open the Scratch program. Scratch starts with a new blank file with a cat **sprite** already created. We're going to make our own characters, so with your mouse, right-click (or on a Mac control-click) on the cat sprite and click **delete** to remove it.

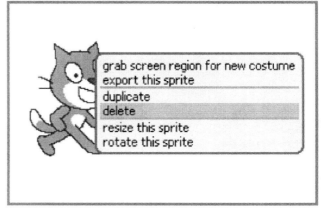

IMPORT YOUR PHOTO

 Click on the Stage in the sprite list, then the **Back-grounds** tab. Click the **Import** button, then your username, and desktop folder to open the desktop, which is where your image is. Click on your image to import. An image of yourself should now fill the background.

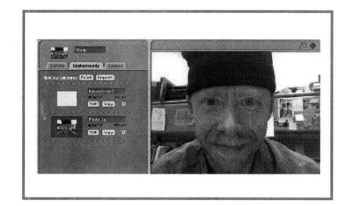

CREATE AND EDIT YOUR SPRITE

 Right-click on the background, select **grab screen region to make new sprite** to get cross-hairs. The cross-hairs will let you grab a section of the background and create a new sprite at the same time.

 Drag crosshairs over one eye. As soon as you let it go you'll have a new sprite — your eye! Move the new eye sprite around to line it up over the background.

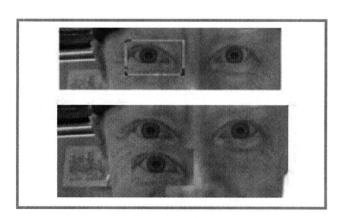

EXPERIMENT WITH PROGRAMMING BLOCKS

6   Click on **Scripts** tab, then on the next window over, click on the **Looks** button and drag out the block. Double-click on block repeatedly and the eye sprite will get bigger and bigger). Reset the eye sprite to its `set size to 100 %` original size by dragging out the *set size to 100%* block and then double-click to reset it.

CREATE A SCRIPT

7   Click on the **Control** button and drag a *repeat* block to the script area, then go to the Motion blocks and drag and attach the *change size by # block* inside the *repeat* block.

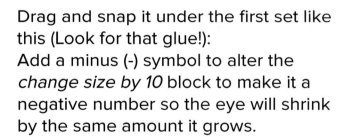

Look for the glue (white line) to appear when trying to insert a block into another block. To reset the size, double-click the *set size to 100%* block.   `set size to 100 %`

8   Copy the entire script by right-clicking on the *repeat* block. Select ***duplicate.***

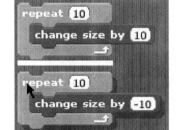

Drag and snap it under the first set like this (Look for that glue!):
Add a minus (-) symbol to alter the *change size by 10* block to make it a negative number so the eye will shrink by the same amount it grows.

9   Drag a *forever* block near the script; it will open-up and surround it.

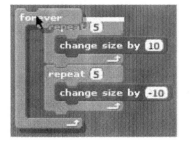

PROGRAM YOUR SPRITE

 10 Drag out a *when green-flag clicked* block. Snap it on top of your script.

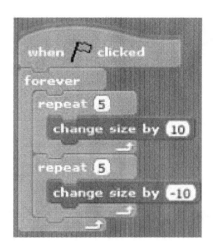

Click the **Green flag** button.
Your eyes should grow and shrink!

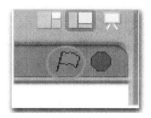

 11 Try animating other features of your face!

Photoface is an easy starting point for introducing and integrating additional tools into your Scratch world. Try incorporating media created in other software and tools into your Photoface project. Use a program like Audacity (sound editing and recording software) to create sounds to import into your project.

CHECK IT OUT!

This document is supported in part by a grant from the Institute of Museum and Library Services. Any views, findings, conclusions or recommendations expressed in this document do not necessarily represent those of the Institute of Museum and Library Services.

Charlotte Mecklenburg Library • Free Library of Philadelphia • Memphis Public Library • Seattle Public Library • Wilmette Public Library

SIMPLE GAME IN SCRATCH

Design your own fun video game using the basic elements of game design in this project for youth (ages 11 – 17) and adult educators. You will create a game where players try and reach a high score or beat a timer that can be tallied using a score, timer, or health variable.

LEARNING GOALS

Start thinking about the game by exploring a theme, a story line, or a goal. You'll draw a main character sprite and decide what objective (another sprite) it will chase or avoid in your game. Finally, decide how to determine when a player wins. This activity is best planned as a formal workshop, not for an open studio. It will also work well as a two (or more) part class, introducing and building on new ideas.

CREATE YOUR GAME CHARACTER AND BACKGROUNDS

Open Scratch and, like earlier projects, delete the cat **sprite**. For the player character, draw a sprite that fits your theme. Either copy the first costume and change it, or draw a new second costume for the sprite if you plan to animate it.

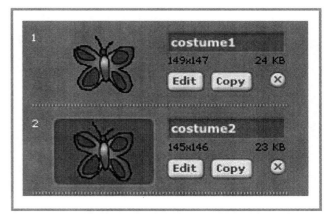

Click on the Stage in the sprite area and create three backgrounds that fit the context of your game. You will need a main game background, a *You Win!* background, and a *Game Over* background. You can re-name each background with a more meaningful name.

Create your objective sprite – this will represent what your player sprite will chase or avoid – a baseball, a dog-bone, or even a flower with nectar.

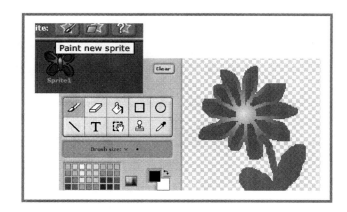

PROGRAM YOUR KEY CONTROLS

Put together scripts for the player sprite that will allow whoever is playing your game to move your player around the screen. The player moves in a specific direction each time one of the arrow keys is pressed.

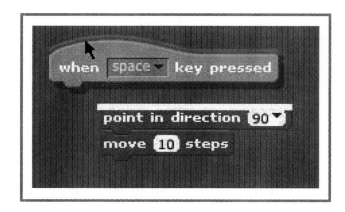

To choose the keys, click the little down arrow next to the word space. This will give you a long drop-down menu of all the keys on the keyboard. We're using **up** arrow, along with **down**, **right**, and **left**.

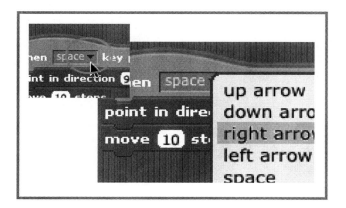

DUPLICATE SCRIPTS

Right-click (or control-click on a Mac) on the top block of your script—this pops up a menu to duplicate or delete the script or block. Click **duplicate** to make a script for for each arrow key.

7 To finish the controls, you'll need to make sure you also change the *point in direction* blocks for each arrow direction.

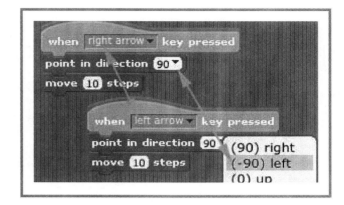

8 Set your player sprite rotation (see the top of the center screen where sprite attributes are displayed) to match your game context. In this case, butterflies don't fly upside down, so you would choose **only face left-right.**

9 If you want your player sprite to animate (and if you've created more costumes), you can add *switch to costume* blocks to the movement scripts. Remember to add them to all of the direction scripts.

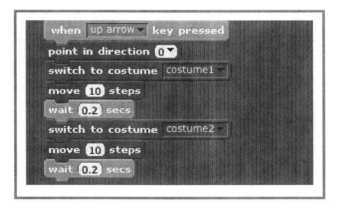

SETTING THINGS UP

10 Now you'll create a script for your objective sprite that sets it in motion when the game begins. First you need to select the objective sprite from the sprites list area.

11 Next, create a script that starts the sprite moving when the green flag is clicked - you can even use the script to send it to random locations.

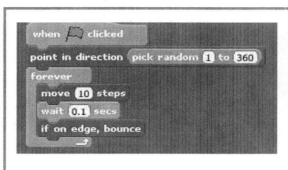

The *go to x and y* block sets the sprite to jump anywhere between the sides, top and bottom of the stage.

12 To make it easier to program what is going to happen between your player sprite and your objective sprite, change their names in the sprite list area.

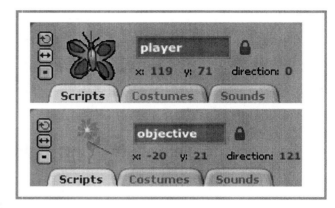

CONDITIONAL STATEMENTS AND VARIABLES

13 In the player sprite script area, create a script with a conditional statement that tells the program what to do if the two sprites come into contact. Find the *touching* block under the **Sensing** button. Choose the objective sprite from the list.

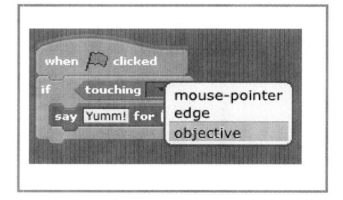

14 Click on the **Variables** button and make a variable named "score." Then revise the script so that it keeps track of when the sprites touch and adds to the score.

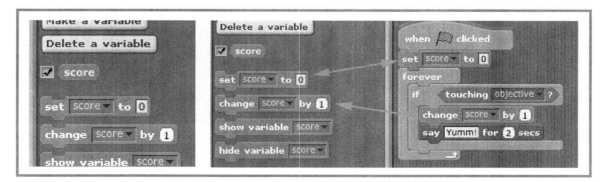

WINNING AND LOSING

 15 The points will continue adding/subtracting as long as the sprites are touching, so you will need to include a way for the sprites to separate immediately. Tell the objective sprite to jump away after it has been caught. Add a conditional to the player sprite script:

 16 Set a limit to the score by adding a new script in the Stage scripts area that says what happens when the game ends. Then when a player reaches a score greater than 9, you can switch to your *You Win* background.

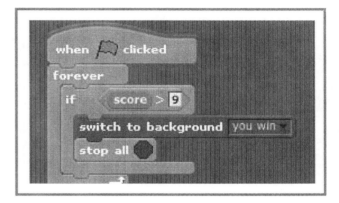

 17 Create a new variable called "timer." Again in the Stage scripts area, create a new timer (or end-of-game) script. The background will change to the *Game Over* background when the time runs out.

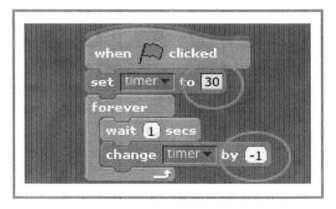

18 Make a conditional statement that checks if the timer has run out (ie., is less than 1), and if it has, switches to the *Game Over* background, then stops the game with a *stop all* block. Put this right under the *change timer by #* block.

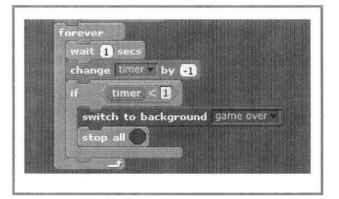

19 To set up the right starting background you'll need one more simple script in the background scripts area. Remember, any script with a *green flag* block will start when it's clicked.

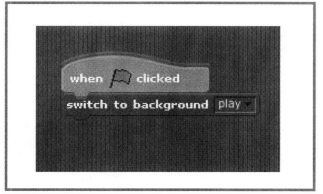

20 This is just a starter Scratch game. You can make it as challenging or as easy as you would like. Be sure to check the game play by having a friend test it as you build it.

After you create your own simple game you will have the ability to create more advanced games like Rock Paper Scissors v2.0 in the Game Examples gallery (http://scratch.mit.edu/galleries/view/25714). These games allow you to explore logic, chance, and game physics.

CHECK IT OUT!

This document is supported in part by a grant from the Institute of Museum and Library Services. Any views, findings, conclusions or recommendations expressed in this document do not necessarily represent those of the Institute of Museum and Library Services.

Charlotte Mecklenburg Library • Free Library of Philadelphia • Memphis Public Library • Seattle Public Library • Wilmette Public Library

DRAWING WITH CIRCLES

Create interesting patterns and rhythms—you'll learn to use Scratch as a programmable drawing tool by integrating the pen-tool blocks along with basic math ideas. This can be a very easy-to-start workshop!

LEARNING GOALS

Explore visual art through the math embodied by "turtle" geometry. Start with simple actions and shapes that repeat to create simple shapes that turn into complex circular and spiral drawings. Introduces the idea of recursion, or "looping."

GET STARTED

Open Scratch; a new blank file with a cat **sprite** will be created. We're going to create a drawing pen tool sprite, so with your mouse, right-click (or on a Mac "control-click") on the cat sprite and click **delete** to remove it.

CREATE A DRAWING SPRITE

Now we'll make our own new sprite by clicking on the **Paintbrush-star** (Paint new sprite) button.

When the Paint Editor window comes up, click on the smallest magnifying glass to zoom out all the way. This lets you see the whole stage (and how big your sprite will be). Choose a small brush size to paint a dot, then click **OK**.

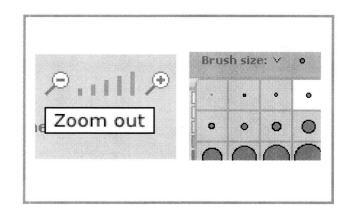

Click on the **Scripts** tab; then, on the next window, click on the **Pen** button and drag out three blocks: *clear, pen down,* and *pen up*. Don't connect these blocks! Just click on the *pen down* block so your dot is ready to draw.

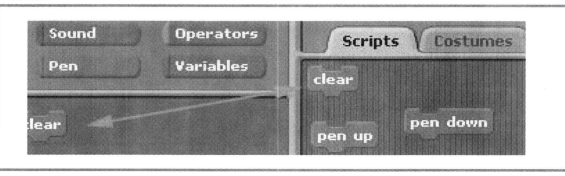

These blocks will be used like buttons—to put the pen down and pull it back up and to clear the screen of any drawn lines. To make sure your pen is down, click the *pen down* block until you see a white outline.

Let's start building a program that will make our dot draw! Click on the **Control** button and grab a *when the green flag is clicked* block to start your program. Click on the **Motion** button, grab a *move 10 steps* block, and connect it to your *green flag* block. Change the number to 50.

Now click the **Green flag** button and the sprite draws 50 steps

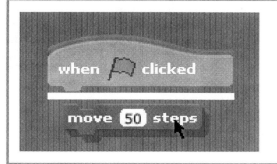

7 Now add a turn to your line, click on the *turn 15 degrees* block, and change it to a big number, "120," then snap it under the *move 50* block; click the green flag to watch your pen move... click it again... and again... and again.

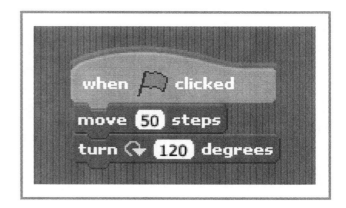

8 What shape did you get? How many times did you click the green flag button to get this shape? Now let's make it draw a larger shape. Just change how many steps it takes by adding 50 more, and then 50 more to the move steps number.

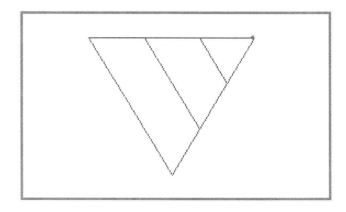

9 Click the clear block in your scripts; it should erase the lines. Now try adding a *repeat 3* block to your script. What happens if you have it repeat more than 3?

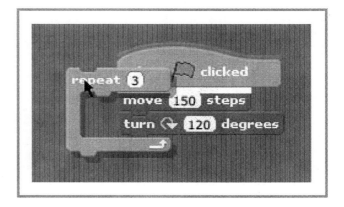

10 This is where it gets really fun. Now that it's automatically drawing triangles, what happens if you add one more small *turn* block after it draws a single triangle?

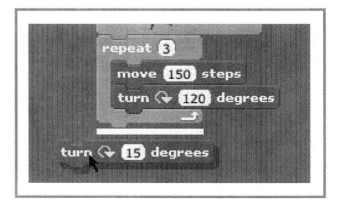

Did you count how many times you clicked to make a full circle with your triangles? Try adding another *repeat* block around your *repeat 3* block.

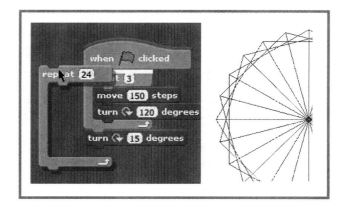

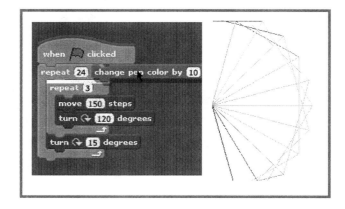

Try changing the size and color. Inserting the *change color by #* and *change pen-size by #* blocks adds interesting effects.

Try using randomness to have your spirals pop up across your stage. Click on the **Operator** button and drag out two *pick random* blocks and another *go to x: y:* block. Set the numbers to roughly the size of your screen. Insert this block at the top of your script. (You can also try using the *random* block with the *change pen color* block.)

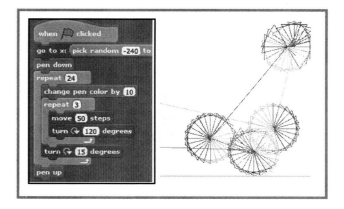

You may notice that as your circles are drawn they drag the pen line from random place to random place. You can add a *pen down* and *pen up* block to the beginning and end of your script.

15 You may even want to have your stage automatically clear each time you run the spirograph. To get it to keep creating spirals you can put a *forever* block around your repeat scripts. Then put the *clear* block right under the *green flag* block.

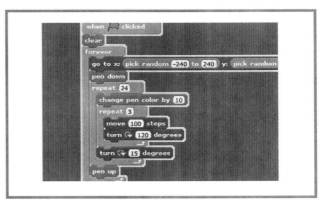

16 This is just the beginning – drawing with Scratch pen has unlimited possibilities!

Happy circle drawing!

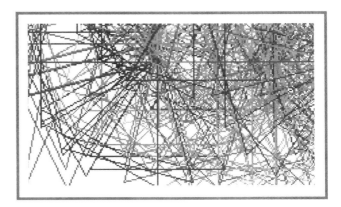

Look at more complex drawing with Scratch; examine the fractal geometry found in the natural world, like ferns, clouds, and seashells and use higher-level mathematics to experiment with creating your own.

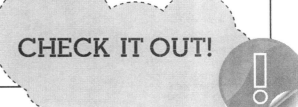

CHECK IT OUT!

This document is supported in part by a grant from the Institute of Museum and Library Services. Any views, findings, conclusions or recommendations expressed in this document do not necessarily represent those of the Institute of Museum and Library Services.

Charlotte Mecklenburg Library • Free Library of Philadelphia • Memphis Public Library • Seattle Public Library • Wilmette Public Library

SCRATCH FORTUNE-TELLER

What is your fortune? What is your wish? This is an intermediate and whimsical project, designed for youth and adult educators, that employs language and humor in Scratch. You will use question-and-answer blocks along with lists to create random fortunes or answers to your deepest questions.

LEARNING GOALS

In Fortune-teller, you'll get an introduction to a number of Scratch elements all in one project. You'll create a number of sprites, and we'll use variables to hold a set of random numbers. The broadcast blocks will let sprites talk to each other and the ask-and-answer will let our fortune-teller talk to the user.

GET STARTED

1 Open Scratch; a new blank file with a cat **sprite** will be created. For this project we'll be creating two more sprites for a total of three. Make the first new sprite by clicking on the **Paintbrush-star** button. This will open the Paint Editor window.

CREATE YOUR 8-BALL

2 For this sprite, draw a large circle using the circle tool. An easy way to make a perfect circle is to hold the shift key down when you draw the circle. Cut a hole in your circle by drawing a smaller circle inside your larger circle.

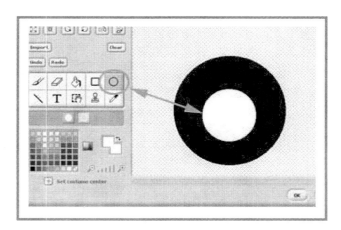

114

3 For the next sprite (your second), click the paintbrush-star button, and from the Paint Editor, use the "T" (font) tool to type a large number 8 in a font you like.

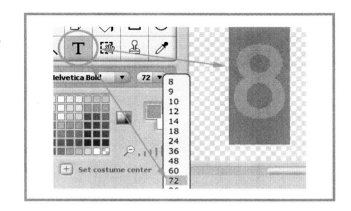

4 Now go back to the cat sprite to edit its costume. To do this, click on the cat in the sprite area; then click on the **Edit** button for its costumes.

5 Next to the copy of the drawing ("costume2" in this case) click the Edit button. Use the magnifying glass to zoom in; then use the eraser to delete the body of the cat so it's just a head. Click **OK** when you are done.

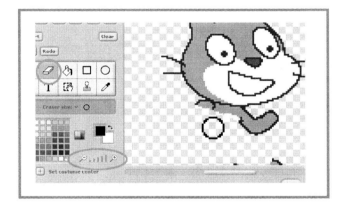

6 On the stage, line up the three sprites on top of each other. Next click on the **Stage** button in the sprites area, then the **Backgrounds** tab. Click the Edit button and use the paint can tool to fill in the background with a color.

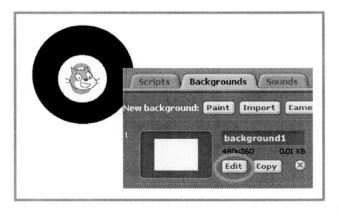

START WORKING WITH VARIABLES

 Go to the blocks area, click the **Variables** button and click on the **Make Variable** button. Name your new variable "Random #." Scratch will create all the variable blocks you need to use this variable.

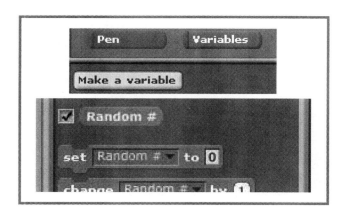

PROGRAM YOUR SPRITES

 Click on your cat sprite; then up on top, above the scripts,

you can click on *sprite1* to rename it "cat." Do this with the ball and the 8. Then go back to the cat sprite's script area.

In the blocks area click the **Control** button and drag out a *when cat clicked* block. You want your program to start when the user clicks on the cat head sprite

 Next go to the Variables blocks and drag out the *Set Random #* Variable block. You can set it to something random, depending on how many answers you have. Click the **Operators** button. Pull out a *pick random # to #* block, change the numbers in the block to "1" and "5."

 Next, we'll hide the cat sprite so that the 8 sprite can appear with a *broadcast* block. After the cat hides, we'll send out a broadcast message to show the 8. To do this you'll have to create a new broadcast message. Drag one out, then click the arrow to add your broadcast message.

11 Your program should look something like this right now:

We'll be adding more to it.

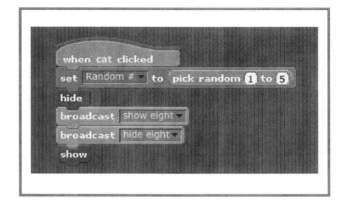

12 While the 8 is showing, the Fortune-Teller is thinking. Let's play a sound to represent that. When you are at the ball sprite, go to **Sounds** tab and click on the **Import** button. Select Bubbles from Effects folder (you can delete the meow).

13 Now add the sound to your script. Don't forget to add some thinking time by inserting a *wait* block.

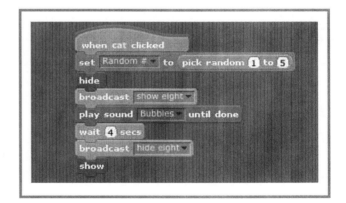

14 Click on the 8 sprite and create some scripts. When the program starts you'll want the 8 to be hidden.

Now you need to have something on the receiving end of your broadcasts from the cat scripts. Create these two scripts:

MAKE YOUR MESSAGES

15 Go back to the cat sprite's scripts and build this script:

You can chose what your 8 ball will say — yes, no, maybe, etc. – with a *say for 2 secs* block.

16 Right-click on top of the script to copy it. Click **duplicate.** Do this to make five copies. Edit each copy to have a different message. Be sure the number of messages equals the number in the variable.

17 Since the variable equals a random number between one and five, you'll use numbers one through five.

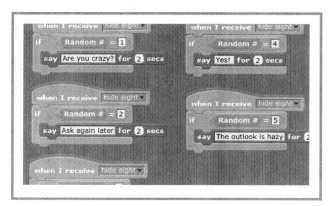

MAKE YOUR MESSAGES

18 Go to the **Sensing** blocks and drag out an *ask _ and wait* block.

Fit it into your cat sprite script like this:
You can fit it between blocks, just wait for the white line to show up where you want to put it.

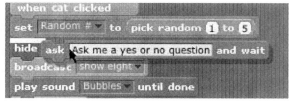

19 This is what your main cat sprite script should look like:

Be sure to test it with a friend to debug any problems

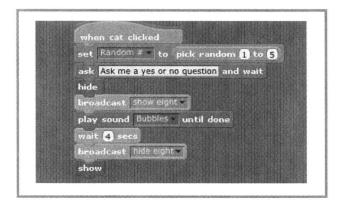

```
when cat clicked
set Random # to pick random 1 to 5
ask Ask me a yes or no question and wait
hide
broadcast show eight
play sound Bubbles until done
wait 4 secs
broadcast hide eight
show
```

 20 Now you're done! Spice up your Fortune-Teller by adding more sounds, changing colors, more messages, or anything else you can think of!

Explore forecasting further by delving into strategy game theory and decision making found in the following projects: **06-Fortuneteller** (http://scratch.mit.edu/projects/keithbraafladt/872798) or **Telephortunes 1.0** (http://scratch.mit.edu/projects/ilmungo/555778).

CHECK IT OUT!

This document is supported in part by a grant from the Institute of Museum and Library Services. Any views, findings, conclusions or recommendations expressed in this document do not necessarily represent those of the Institute of Museum and Library Services.

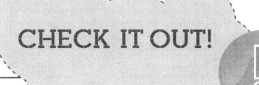

Charlotte Mecklenburg Library • Free Library of Philadelphia • Memphis Public Library • Seattle Public Library • Wilmette Public Library

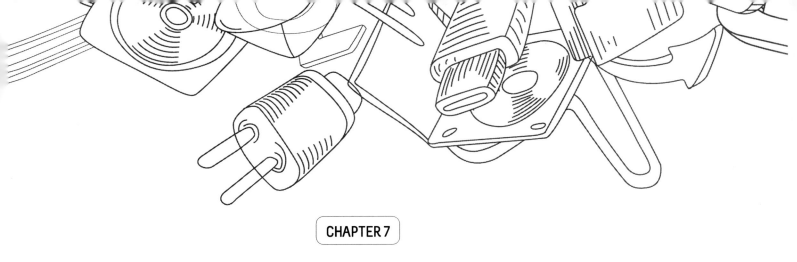

CHAPTER 7

Resources

Checklist of equipment and supplies for Scratch-based programs

- ☐ computers
- ☐ flash drives
- ☐ power strips or extension cords
- ☐ scanner
- ☐ drawing tablets
- ☐ digital cameras
- ☐ batteries
- ☐ PICO boards
- ☐ sensor boards
- ☐ Lego WeDo
- ☐ software downloads
- ☐ drawing paper
- ☐ pencils, markers, pens

Understanding and using Scratch

Books

Badger, Michael. *Scratch 1.4 Beginner's Guide.* London: Packt Publishing, 2009.

Ford Jr., Jerry Lee. *Scratch Programming for Teens.* Ann Arbor: Course Technology—a division of Cengage Learning, 2009.

Websites

Learn Scratch. https://mywebspace.wisc.edu/dhawk/scratch/.

Media MashUp. www.mediamashup.ning.com.

Scratch Beginner's Guide. www.scratchguide.com/.

Scratch Cards. http://info.scratch.mit.edu/Support/Scratch_Cards.

ScratchEd. www.scratch-ed.org

Scratch Getting Started Guide. http://info.scratch.mit.edu/sites/infoscratch.media
.mit.edu/files/file/ScratchGettingStartedv14.pdf.

Scratch Reference Guide. http://info.scratch.mit.edu/Support/Reference_Guide_1.4.

Scratch Resources. http://resources.scratchr.org/.

Scratch Wiki. http://wiki.scratch.mit.edu/wiki/Scratch_Wiki.

Video Tutorials. http://info.scratch.mit.edu/Video_Tutorials.

Learn more about libraries and literacy in the 21st century

Institute of Museum and Library Services. "Museums, Libraries, and 21st Century
Skills." www.imls.gov/about/21stCSkills.shtm.

Jones-Kavalier, Barbara, and Suzanne Flannigan. "Connecting
the Digital Dots: Literacy of the 21st Century." *Educause
Quarterly* 29, no. 2 (2006). www.educause.edu/
EDUCAUSE+Quarterly/EDUCAUSEQuarterlyMagazineVolum/
ConnectingtheDigitalDotsLitera/157395.

MacArthur Foundation. "Digital Media and Learning." http://digitallearning
.macfound.org/site/c.enJLKQNlFiG/b.2029271/k.98D4/MacArthur_Series
.htm. Metiri Group. "enGauge 21st Century Skills." www.metiri.com/features
.html.

Partnership for 21st Century Skills. www.p21.org.

Learn more about the development of Scratch

Peppler, Kylie et al. *The Computer Clubhouse: Constructionism and Creativity in Youth
Communities.* New York: Teacher's College Press, 2009.

Resnick, Mitchel. Website: http://web.media.mit.edu/~mres/.

Scratch research is compiled at http://info.scratch.mit.edu/Research.

Learn more about children, education, and technology

Ackerman, Edith. "Piaget's Constructivism, Papert's Constructionism: What's the
Difference?" http://learning.media.mit.edu/content/publications/EA.Piaget%20
_%20Papert.pdf.

Papert, Seymour. *Mindstorms.* New York: Basic Books, 1980.

Papert, Seymour. Website: www.papert.org/.

Piaget, Jean. *The Psychology of the Child.* New York: Basic Books, 2000.

Search Institute. "Developmental Assets." www.search-institute.org/developmental
-assets.

Wood, Kay C et al. "Piaget's Stages of Cognitive Development." In Emerging
Perspectives on Learning, Teaching and Technology, edited by Michael Orey.
Bloomington, IN: Association for Educational Communications and Technology,
2001. http://projects.coe.uga.edu/epltt/index.php?title=Piaget's_Stages.

Technology programs in public libraries

Matthias, Cynthia, and Christy Mulligan. 2010. "Hennepin County Library's Teen
Tech Squad Youth Leadership and Technology Free-for-All." *Young Adult
Library Services* 8, no. 2 (2010).

Myers, Brian. "Imagine > Invent > Program > Share: A Library-Hosted Computer
Club Promotes 21st Century Literacy Skills." *Computers in Libraries,* 29, no. 3
(2008): 36–40.

Romero, Juan Suarez. "Library Programming with LEGO MINDSTORMS, Scratch,
and PicoCricket: Analysis of Best Practices for Public Libraries." *Computers in
Libraries* 30, no. 1 (2010): 16–45

Free and low-cost software for technology programs

All of the software and hardware listed here can be used on Macintosh or Windows.

Alice and Storytelling Alice are 3-D programming software developed by Carnegie
Mellon and free to download and use. Storytelling Alice is designed specifically
for middle school students. www.alice.org.

Artrage 2.5 is a low-cost drawing program and has a free version with limited capability.
The free version has enough features to make it a good drawing program for kids
who want more than Scratch's painting toolbox offers. www.artrage.com.

Audacity is a free audio editor. Kids can use it to edit sound files and incorporate into
Scratch projects. http://.audacity.sourceforge.net.

Comic Life is low cost and has a demo version you can download to try for free. Kids
love using it to make high-quality comics and storyboards. http://plasq.com/
products/comiclife/.

GameMaker is a free download that can be used to create more advanced games. www
.yoyogames.com/gamemaker/.

Gimp is free image manipulation software. Files can be imported to Scratch projects. www.gimp.org.

Lego WeDo can be programmed using Scratch blocks and used to create projects that interact with the physical world, such as puppets or controllers. www.lego.com/education/school/default.asp?locale=2057&pagename=WD_Con&12id=3_2&13id=3_2_1&14id=3_2_1_1.

Picasa is free photo editing software that can be used to edit photos and to import or create Scratch backgrounds or sprites. http://picasa.google.com.

Playful Invention Company has low-cost sensor boards that can be programmed from Scratch. The sensors allow Scratch projects to have an impact on, and respond to, changes in the physical world—sound, light and motion. www.picocricket.com/picoboard.html.

SAM Animation has a free demo version that kids can download and use to easily learn techniques for stop-motion animation. www.samanimation.com/.

StarLogoTNG is free modeling and simulation software developed by the Scheller Teacher Education Program at the Massachusetts Institute of Technology. http://education.mit.edu/projects/starlogo-tng.

Bibliography

Albright, Meagan et al. "The Evolution of Early Literacy: A History of Best Practices." *Children and Libraries* (Spring 2009): 13–18.

American Library Association. "Number of Libraries in the United States." Fact Sheet 1. www.ala.org/ala/professionalresources/libfactsheets/alalibraryfactsheet01.cfm.

Arnold, Renea and Nell Colburn. "The (Really) Big Six: Early Literacy Skills." *School Library Journal* (November 1, 2008). http:www.schoollibraryjournal.com/article/CA6610494.html.

Bertot, John Carlo et al. "Libraries Connect Communities 3: Public Library Funding and Technology Access Study 2007–2009." www.ala.org/ala/research/initiatives/plftas/index.cfm.

"Conceptual Economy." *Wikipedia.* http://en.wikipedia.org/wiki/Conceptual_economy.

Corporation for Public Broadcasting. "Formal versus Informal Education." In *Enhancing Education: A Children's Producer's Guide.* 2002. http://enhancinged.wgbh.org/started/what/formal.html.

Coy, Peter. "The Creative Economy." *Businessweek Online* (August 28, 2000). www.businessweek.com/2000/00_35/b3696002.htm.

Ellingson, Jo Ann. "21st Century Literacy: Libraries Must Lead." *American Libraries* 29, no. 11 (December 1998): 52–53.

Gullett, Matt (independent library consultant), in discussion with the author, April 13, 2010, Seattle, WA.

Haggstrom, Britt Marie, ed. "The Role of Libraries in Lifelong Learning." Final report of the International Federation of Library Associations and Institutions, 2004. http://archive.ifla.org/VII/s8/proj/Lifelong-LearningReport.pdf.

Hsi, Sherry. "Conceptualizing Learning from the Everyday Activities of Digital Kids." *International Journal of Science Education* 29, no. 12 (October 2007): 1509–1529.

Ito, Mizuko et al. *Hanging Out, Messing Around and Geeking Out: Living and Learning with New Media.* Cambridge, MA: MIT Press, 2009.

Mackenzie, Christine. "Emerging Themes for Public Libraries Looking Forward." *APLIS* (Australasian Public Libraries and Information Services) (December 2009): 184–189.

MacLean, Judy. "Library Preschool Storytimes: Developing Early Literacy Skills in Children." 2008. www.ed.psu.edu/goodlinginstitute/pdf/fam_lit_cert_stud_work/Judy%20MacLean%20 Library%20Preschool%20Storytimes.pdf.

New England Foundation for the Arts. "Strengthening the Creative Economy." www.nefa.org/what _we_do/strengthening_creative_economy.

OCLC, Inc. "How Libraries Stack Up: 2010." www.oclc.org/reports/stackup/.

Peppler, Kylie et al. *The Computer Clubhouse: Constructionism and Creativity in Youth Communities.* New York: Teacher's College Press, 2009.

Phipps, Molly. Organizational Change Interviews. 2009. www.hclib.org/extranet/MediaMashup/ MediaMashUp_OrgChg0409.pdf.

"Piaget's Theory of Cognitive Development." *Wikipedia.* http://en.wikipedia.org/wiki/Theory_of _cognitive_development

Pink, Daniel. *A Whole New Mind.* London: Riverhead Books, 2005.

Resnick, Mitchel. "All I Really Need to Know (About Creative Thinking) I Learned (by Studying How Children Learn) in Kindergarten," in *Proceedings of the Creativity and Cognition Conference,* Washington, DC, June 2007.

Resnick, Mitchel. "Learning by Designing." http://info.scratch.mit.edu/sites/infoscratch.media.mit.edu/ docs/learning-by-designing.pdf.

Resnick, Mitchel et al. "Scratch Programming for All." *Communications of the ACM* 52, no. 11 (November 2009): 60–67.

Romero, Juan Suarez. "Library Programming with LEGO MINDSTORMS, Scratch, and PicoCricket: Analysis of Best Practices for Public Libraries." *Computers in Libraries* 30, no. 1 (2010): 16–45.

Rusk, Natalie et al. "21st Century Learning Skills." http://info.scratch.mit.edu/sites/infoscratch.media .mit.edu/docs/Scratch-21stCenturySkills.pdf.

Santrock, J. W. *A Topical Approach to Life Span Development.* New York: McGraw-Hill, 2008.

Southwick-Trask, Lesley. "Building New Skills for the Knowledge Economy." *Business Communications Review* 26, no. 2 (February 1996): 28.

YALSA. "Risky Business." Virtual President's Panel, 2010. www.yalsa.ala.org/ yalsapresident2010/?page_id=9.

Index

You may also be interested in

LISTENING TO LEARN
Audiobooks Supporting Literacy
SHARON GROVER AND LIZETTE D. HANNEGAN

This resource connects audiobooks with K–12 curricula and demonstrates how the format can support national learning standards and literacy skills.

ISBN: 978-0-8389-1107-5
200 PAGES / 6" x 9"

DIVERSITY IN YOUTH LITERATURE
EDITED BY
JAMIE CAMPBELL NAIDOO
AND SARAH PARK

ISBN: 978-0-8389-1143-3

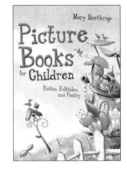

PICTURE BOOKS FOR CHILDREN
MARY NORTHRUP

ISBN: 978-0-8389-1144-0

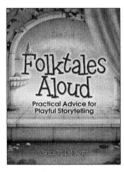

FOLKTALES ALOUD
JANICE M. DEL NEGRO

ISBN: 978-0-8389-1135-8

GRAPHIC NOVELS IN YOUR SCHOOL LIBRARY
JESSE KARP,
ILLUSTRATED BY RUSH KRESS

ISBN: 978-0-8389-1089-4

MULTICULTURAL STORYTIME MAGIC
KATHY MacMILLAN AND
CHRISTINE KIRKER

ISBN: 978-0-8389-1142-6

CHILDREN'S PROGRAMMING MONTHLY SUBSCRIPTION
26 ISSUES FOR ONLY $50!

ITEM NUMBER: 1541-8826

CPSIA information can be obtained at www.ICGtesting.com
Printed in the USA
LVOW030505170212

269133LV00007B/2/P